Exploring the Unknown

Exploring the Unknown

MYSTERIES IN AMERICAN ARCHAEOLOGY

Sharon S. McKern

PRAEGER PUBLISHERS
New York · Washington · London

PRAEGER PUBLISHERS
111 Fourth Avenue, New York, N.Y. 10003, U.S.A.
5, Cromwell Place, London SW7 2JL, England

Published in the United States of America in 1972
by Praeger Publishers, Inc.

Second printing, 1973

© 1972 by Praeger Publishers, Inc.

Library of Congress Catalog Card Number: 76–168343

Printed in the United States of America

Contents

List of Illustrations

9

Figures

Acknowledgments

No book is the product of a single author—and this one grew because it was amply fed with ideas and suggestions contributed by those who share my fascination with the mysteries of the buried past.

I am indebted to Robert E. Stone, who shared bibliographies and photographs relating to the Mystery Hill site; to T. Dale Stewart, who answered my frequent cries for information with unfailing patience; and to Legrand H. Clegg II, who introduced me to the realities of black-white dialogue and who taught me a great deal more than is contained in this book. As always, I am grateful to Praeger editors Mary Louise Birmingham and Martha King; their responsiveness and good will took much of the work out of authorship for me.

Special thanks go to two magazine editors whose interest in prehistory led to the publication of numerous articles—mine and others—dealing with archaeological discoveries: Portions of Chapters 3 and 5 were initially published in article form by *Science Digest* magazine (© The Hearst Corporation, 1970); the material revised and expanded here is included with the permission of Richard F. Dempewolff, one of my favorite editors. Sections of Chapter 7 were drawn from my article originally published by *Mankind* magazine (© Mankind Publishing Company, 1970); my thanks go to *Mankind*'s energetic and knowledgeable editor Raymond F. Locke.

But most important—my gratitude to Tom McKern, my husband and closest friend, whose wisdom and love and patience make mine the best of all possible worlds.

Lawrence, Kansas
January, 1972

Exploring the Unknown

1

The Earliest Americans

What happened in the Americas before the coming of Columbus?
For the gold-hungry Europeans who swarmed into the New World
early in the sixteenth century, the question was irrelevant. There
was gold there, and jade. Vast lands awaited exploration and ex-
ploitation. The soil was rich and fertile; the coastal waters teemed
with fish. Stingerless bees bred in the hollows of trees and yielded
the purest honey. Salt, the most revered of trade commodities,
was abundant.

The nations of western Europe, first to reach the New World,
rushed to reap the rewards of discovery. Back across the Atlantic
explorers carried their prizes, including dozens of strange American foods that would revolutionize life in the Old World. The
white potato fast became a European staple. Kidney and lima
beans, corn, tomatoes, and turkeys provided cheap new means of
feeding the growing population of Europe. Chocolate and chili

peppers, exciting new taste sensations, found instant acceptance. Soon tobacco and cotton turned quick profits in an expanding world market. Little wonder that, for the initial European invaders and for the millions who followed in their wake, American history began in 1492.

But Columbus did not land on a deserted beach. His entry into the New World brought him face to face with peoples who boasted a history in the Americas thousands of years long—a history that is lost, for the most part, in the vastness of time. As far as we know, the first Americans came not in ships but on foot, across the Bering Strait. At least 38,000 years ago (but perhaps as early as 70,000 B.C.), loosely organized bands of prehistoric hunters crossed from eastern Siberia into arctic Alaska on the trail of roaming game: the musk ox, the woolly mammoth, the caribou, and the bison. They were nomads, primitives whose material culture was so meager that it lacked even the simple bow and arrow. They carried little more than a few crude stone weapons and had a remarkable skill, born of necessity, for using these against the fierce and powerful animals of that time.

These were marginal peoples, splintered groups of ice-age Asiatics who penetrated the Americas before the spread of crucial Old World inventions such as the wheel. They had not learned to make pottery or to work metals. They had never seen a city. They had no notion of agriculture and had no domesticated animals save the dog—and the earliest immigrants lacked even that companion.

Their goal was not to escape the bitter cold of Siberia, for they had no way of knowing what lands lay ahead. Intent upon tracking the roving game herds, they were unaware that they passed into a new, uninhabited continent. They simply moved their camp sites in accordance with the feeding cycles of the huge Pleistocene mammals on which they depended for food and hides. As the herds moved slowly and instinctively toward new grazing grounds, the hunters and their families plodded doggedly after.

The Bering Strait offered an accessible—almost unavoidable— route into the New World. Even today, the shores of Siberia and Alaska are separated by no more than 56 air miles. Thanks to the strategically located Diomede Islands, the longest unbroken span of water measures half that distance. On a clear day, one can stand on the coastal tundra of Alaska and sight with ease the shores of eastern Siberia.

At the time of the initial Asiatic migrations, extensive glaciation had lowered sea levels by several hundred feet, exposing the continental shelves and revealing a wide, plainlike land bridge linking Asia with Alaska.

It was not a constant land connection. In warmer periods, water from melting glaciers raised sea levels to narrow or submerge the land link. But, in colder periods, moisture evaporated from the seas to fall as snow on the great land masses—and huge quantities of the oceans' waters were locked up in immense ice-age glaciers. Then the land bridge emerged anew, allowing random and sporadic waves of immigrants to cross. In effect, the Bering Strait passage served as a valve or drawbridge regulating the flow of animal and human migration into the New World. At its maximum exposure, the land connection measured 600 to 1,000 miles in width, easy passage for hunters who tracked slow-moving game herds. During most of the final glacial advance, the area around the Bering Strait escaped the massive ice sheet that ripped across so much of the North American continent. Ice and snow were at a minimum, blanketing only the upper ridges. Warm Pacific currents lapped at the southern edges of the dry-land passage. Here, vegetation grew—soft grasses, mosses, lichens, and heaths—sustaining the dispersed herds that moved freely from one continent to the other and, sometimes, back again.

At no time did there occur a single wave of human migration. Available game would have been too scattered to support large numbers of people living and traveling together. And the rate of migration must have been slow, averaging no more than a few miles per generation. Still, family units and small hunting bands trickled in over a span of thousands of years.

Generation succeeded generation. Old people would die along the way. But women would give birth, and younger, stronger legs would take up the uncharted journey.

Many may have wandered off the grazing trails to perish in the icy wilderness to the north. There is no record of their passing.

Figure 1. Major migration routes into the New World.

Others leaked back into Siberia, unaware that they had walked upon the face of a vast new land mass.

But others, funneling in through Alaska, came upon the Yukon and Mackenzie rivers, where fresh water and big game abounded. The ice-free corridor of the Yukon Valley beckoned, luring the grazing herds and the men who fed on them to travel deep into the continent's lush grasslands.

Food was plentiful and the climate benign south of the arctic icecap. The earliest immigrants multiplied and spread, pushed on into new lands by their own expanding numbers or displaced by later arrivals from Asia. A few filtered down through California and out onto the coastal islands. Many groups turned to the east, skirting the great open plains to melt into the dense woodlands beyond. Still others spilled southward, penetrating deep into Mexico and Central America. A few crossed the narrow passage through the land we know today as Panama to enter South America.

Eventually, America's earliest inhabitants traversed both continents of the New World, reaching by 11,000 years ago Tierra del Fuego, at the very tip of South America—and the end of the longest journey in prehistory.

About 10,000 years ago the sea reclaimed the Bering Strait land passage for the last time. Occasional late-comers—including the ancestors of all modern Eskimo groups—would cross on winter's ice or risk the watery gap by kayak. But for the most part the Americas were once again sealed off from the rest of the world.

The Asian immigrants never became a homogeneous population in the New World. Entering as they did in small bands, over tens of thousands of years, they represented different branches of a prehistoric Asian race. As nomads, they led a tribal existence apart from other human groups.

Tribal differences both physical and cultural intensified as the roving bands of hunters moved into widely separated regions of the spacious New World. Members of different tribes shared only the most general physical resemblances. These—dark eyes, straight hair, prominent cheek bones, and a distinctive form of dentition— were strong Mongoloid traits that denote a common origin on the Asian mainland.

Differences in life style were extreme. North America's original human inhabitants learned to exploit diverse environments. Some hunted in the cool northern forests. Others settled along the rivers and sea coasts, taking their sustenance from marine life. Still others gathered wild roots and berries in the dense pine woods or trapped small animals in the arid deserts of the American Southwest. Slowly, life became more sedentary. Each tribe laid claim to its own territory and developed unique customs and life ways in unconscious adaptation to its surroundings.

By the time Columbus reached New World shores, there was no one type of American Indian. Some were savages. Some were empire builders. Others had vanished completely centuries before the arrival of the earliest Europeans and had left behind—in stone and bone—vague but tantalizing clues to their existence.

In North America, the men who came in sixteenth-century ships met tribes of primitive hunters who lived a precarious Stone Age existence. Most had mastered the art of farming, but theirs was a crude and limited agriculture, on which they could not depend exclusively. They stalked game when it was available and, when it was not, scrounged for wild roots and seeds to see them through the lean months of winter.

In Central and South America, however, discovery brought the Europeans into contact with peoples of amazing sophistication. In the fertile Mexican highlands, they came upon an extraordinary civilization comparable in many ways to that of anicent Egypt. This was Tenochtitlán, the treasure-laden Aztec capital that was five times the size of sixteenth-century London.

Here great, tiered pyramids and spectacular stone temples loomed against the sky. There were zoos, parks, ball courts, schools, both religious and secular, and well-regulated markets where vendors hawked the varied wares and products of a rich and extensive nation. Blood-splattered stone altars, stained by frequent human sacrifices, told of a fierce and demanding Indian religion so bloodthirsty that it horrified the most hardened of Old World explorers. In vivid contrast, Tenochtitlán's civil and other secular affairs were tended with measured prudence and solicitude. A corps of administrative officials presided over an orderly system of justice, operated a trained police force, and collected—

according to ability to pay—yearly tribute from outlying villages.

This magnificent Mexican city, described by Cortes as the most beautiful in the world, seemed to ride atop the waves of Lake Texcoco. And it was, in fact, built upon a marshy island in the middle of that lake. Massive stone causeways with removable wooden bridges linked the capital with the mainland. Canals served as streets, as in Venice, and strange "floating" gardens yielded up to *seven* annual crops.

Other American wonders awaited the invading Europeans. In the tropical rain forests of Guatemala and Honduras, energetic explorers found mysterious deserted cities and fallen stone monuments, all ornately carved. These, half-hidden by the encroaching jungle, were the ruins of a brilliant native civilization whose birth predated Tenochtitlán and whose decline predated Columbus. This was the home of the classic Maya.

But it was in Peru that the conquistadors found the largest and most dazzling of all New World civilizations. Here they marveled at a vast and complex native welfare state ruled by the aristocratic Incas. Peruvian agriculture, supervised by experts trained and supported by the state, was highly productive: Millions of acres of arid desert land had been cultivated with the aid of extensive systems of irrigation. Tiers of agricultural terraces transformed the rugged mountain slopes into fertile gardens. Stone-lined aqueducts carried clear water from mountain springs into the Inca cities, supplying public baths and fountains. There were paved roads, suspension bridges, and buildings of perfect symmetry—surpassing in size and sheer splendor the grandest structures of sixteenth-century Europe. Carved statuary and textiles—the finest in the world—abounded. Cuzco, capital of the Inca Empire, glittered with treasure. And in the homes of the living were enshrined the golden-masked mummies of the Peruvian dead.

Here, in Central and South America, were peoples who devised a complex calendar more exact than our own and a numbering system that surpassed that of the ancient Greeks. Here were peoples savage enough to practice blood sacrifice but learned enough to map the skies, to distinguish stars from planets, and to predict with astonishing accuracy the times of solar eclipses. Here were peoples woefully ignorant of their own past but remarkable for their unparalleled achievements in architecture, mathematics, astronomy, art, and engineering.

The conquistadors had come for gain, not to ponder the past. And as they pressed on toward total conquest—burning native books, looting tombs, defacing monuments—they gave no thought to the preservation of these unique native cultures. The Spanish had come for gold and glory; intent upon their search for these, they had no time to waste on native histories.

For the natives of Mexico and Peru, the Europeans brought disaster. Soon warfare, slavery, famine, and disease took their ugly toll. Within the span of a few decades, the remarkable empires of Central and South America collapsed into ruins, their histories unrecorded.

Early Spanish chronicles, it is true, describe sixteenth-century life in Mexico and Peru, but these are biased and often superficial accounts penned by men more concerned with glorifying conquest than with preserving the past.

Neither the Aztecs nor the Mayas had true written histories as we know them. But both boasted native "books" or manuscripts known today as codices. These were made from long strips of pounded tree bark or deerskin that were folded accordian-style. Individual "pages" were filled with colorful pictographs reminiscent of modern comic books or, in the case of the Mayas, with elaborate hieroglyphics. Apparently, the codices were never intended for general use. They were reserved for the upper learned classes—priests, noblemen, astronomers, and scribes—whose responsibilities included matters of science and state. Unfortunately, none of the known pre-Columbian codices are essentially historical in nature; most appear to have served as guides to ritual and astrological procedure, although archaeologists agree that the Mayas must have recorded their history in hieroglyphic manuscripts.

Only a handful of pre-Columbian Aztec writings and just three Maya codices escaped the book-burnings so zealously conducted by Spanish priests and conquistadors—but these are difficult to decipher, and those that can be translated are filled with myth and legend. Neither Spanish nor native accounts tell how the advanced New World civilizations developed. None shed light on the lives of the earliest Americans, those who lived and died centuries before.

Fortunately, there are other kinds of records to tell of life in the prehistoric New World. Ruins, relics, mummies, and bones: these are keys to an archaeological alphabet whose letters spell out the story of man and his works in pre-Columbian America.

The first New World archaeologists were as adventurous, in their own ways, as the conquistadors who came in the wake of Columbus. They began their investigations when archaeology was still an infant science, lacking the sophisticated tools and techniques of modern times. The ruins and artifacts they sought to examine were located, more often than not, in remote and inaccessible regions. The natives on whom they depended for labor and guidance were neither reliable nor consistently friendly.

Still, relics of vanished tribes and lost civilizations make powerful lures for those who seek to reconstruct a record of life in the distant past. Beginning early in the nineteenth century, archaeologists both amateur and professional began to probe America's ancient ruins. In 1839, John Lloyd Stephens and Frederick Catherwood set out to explore abandoned Maya cities in the snake-infested jungles of Central America. They landed in Guatemala in the midst of a chaotic three-way civil war and were promptly jailed by a band of drunken soldiers. Fortunately, the two men won their release on the following morning and continued their explorations, carefully dodging rival armies. Later, Stephens' exuberant writings and Catherwood's intricate sketches brought the mysterious Maya culture to the attention of the outside world and triggered a wave of archaeological exploration in Middle America.

In 1885, Edward H. Thompson began his investigations at Chichén Itzá, in Yucatán. He risked his life diving into a steep-walled, sludge-filled Maya well and later battled a 14-foot boa constrictor for the right to enter an ancient tomb. But he survived both escapades to devote forty years of his life to the exploration of scattered antiquities in Central America.

In 1911, Hiram Bingham led an expedition into the unmapped interior of southern Peru, across the rapids of the mighty Urubamba River, and up the sheer-faced sides of the Andes. Near the top of a rugged 19,300-foot mountain, Bingham found the city of

Machu Picchu—an Inca fortress unknown to the outside world for more than 350 years. Never reached by sixteenth-century explorers, this remarkable city remains much as its inhabitants left it centuries ago.

Such spectacular discoveries are rare in archaeology, where sweat is a more common companion than adventure. Much of the work of archaeology is sheer drudgery: crawling into dusty caves or sifting through tons of ancient soil in search of some fragmentary relics. Sometimes, whole cities and vast prehistoric cemeteries are excavated. But, more often, archaeologists make do with smaller prizes. They follow the trail of the earliest American immigrants by digging for bits of broken stone weapons or shattered mammoth bones—or they seek to pinpoint the origin of New World agriculture by scouring the continent for tiny fossilized grains of corn pollen. Relics and bones rescued from buried temples, pyramids, tombs, burial mounds, and prehistoric rubbish heaps add a few more pieces to the puzzle that is the American past. However meager, these clues continue to lure men and women into the field.

Over a century of exploration and excavation, archaeologists have used such clues to reconstruct much of America's prehistory. Our library shelves are lined with volumes describing the achievements of the Aztecs, Incas, and Mayas. Museum collections bulge with skeletons, mummies, and artifacts painstakingly collected from prehistoric graves. And more is learned each year as archaeologists continue to resurrect buried cities and to dig for fossilized bones.

But the American story is far from complete. Huge gaps remain in the archaeological record. The jumbled puzzle resists solution; the past guards its secrets jealously.

Some evidence will never be found. Buried deep in the earth or hidden from sight by tangled vegetation, many ruins and relics may forever escape detection. Others will fall victim to the raging course of technological progress. In 1969, UNESCO stepped in to rescue the ancient temples of Philae, in Cairo, which were threatened with destruction as a result of the Aswân Dam; in the United States, salvage archaeologists work feverishly to save American treasures similarly threatened. But each year, dozens of potentially productive archaeological sites are inundated by the waters of new dams and reservoirs. Dozens more are obliterated by bulldozers because they lie in the path of highway construction.

Many clues to America's prehistory are simply lost; they have decayed completely. Others are carted away by amateur pot-hunters and treasure-seekers. An abundance of evidence remains, of course. Hundreds of known sites have been excavated, yielding up a wealth of data. And thousands of additional sites have been located. These stand silent, their secrets intact, awaiting their turn. There are ruins and artifacts sufficient to keep American archaeologists busy for another hundred years.

But even where prehistoric evidence is plentiful, mysteries abound. For only a fraction of a people's history can be reconstructed through analysis of its physical remains. Many relics give no hint of their prehistoric purposes. And some clues pose more questions than they answer.

Archaeologists cannot yet explain the Nazca lines—the gigantic drawings etched into the Peruvian desert by a prehistoric people who, having no aerial vantage point, could never view their own craftsmanship.

Scholars puzzle over the 12-ton stone spheres that litter the jungle underbrush of Costa Rica. Who carved these immense stone balls? When and why?

Who was the boy whose frozen, preserved body—surrounded by bright feathers and toy llamas—was found high atop Lead Mountain in Chile? Did this child serve as an emissary to the Inca gods? Who carried him there? Who buried him alive in his isolated tomb?

Anthropologists marvel over trepanned skulls from Peru—the strangely incised human skulls that tell of prehistoric brain surgeries. Why did ancient Indians permit their surgeons to cut, with crude stone knives, into the living skull? How is it that so many patients survived this radical and risky surgery?

Who can unravel the riddle of the Maya, that enigmatic race of Indians who raised majestic stone cities in the heart of Guatemala's inhospitable Petén Jungle and then suddenly abandoned them in the ninth century A.D.?

And who can explain the baffling hints, recurring again and

again across the hemisphere, of unknown Old World explorers who may have sailed to American shores centuries before Columbus or Leif Ericson?

These are but a few of the unsolved mysteries that haunt those who try to peer into the American past. We will explore the most intriguing of them in the following pages.

But do not look for answers here: This is a book of archaeological mysteries and of the people who have sought to solve them. Some of them are riddles that will never be unraveled.

2

Machu Picchu: Lost City in the Clouds

High on a mountain saddle between two jagged peaks in the most inaccessible region of the Peruvian Andes lies a granite city built by the Incas and abandoned more than 400 years ago.

Its name is lost in time. Tourists, moved by the city's beauty, call it the "jewel of Peru." Archaeologists call it Machu Picchu, after the mountain it straddles.

Here steep garden terraces, now carpeted in grass, cling to the sides of the rugged Andean slopes. Great stone walls and rock-lined ditches guard the deserted citadel. Inside, clusters of in-geniously built houses and dozens of ancient temples stand almost as if their inhabitants had abandoned them only yesterday. Inca aqueducts still carry fresh water from nearby springs to replenish city fountains.

Cuzco, once capital of the vast Inca Empire and later head-quarters for Pizarro's conquering troops, lies only 60 miles away.

But the Spanish conquistadors never found Machu Picchu. Tucked away among sheer-faced cliffs and blocked by a nearly impenetrable jungle, this mountain refuge was lost to the outside world for more than 350 years.

No records survive to tell of the city's founding, or why it was abandoned. And the ruins on Machu Picchu Mountain might have remained undetected had it not been for the determined efforts of a single young scholar bent on locating the last sanctuary of the vanquished Incas. Hiram Bingham, then an energetic assistant professor at Yale University, was drawn to the region by tantalizing rumors of a fabulous lost city located somewhere to the northwest of Cuzco. Riding muleback, Bingham followed hillside trail after trail and found no ruins of importance. Then, in July of 1911, he set out on a final expedition. He was accompanied this time by two scientist friends, a few native guides, and a Peruvian police sergeant assigned to protect the foolhardy Americans.

Six days out of Cuzco, Bingham's party made camp on the banks of the Urubamba River. They encountered a Quechua Indian innkeeper who told them of extensive native ruins in the immediate vicinity—on top of the peak called Huayna Picchu and on the adjacent mountain, Machu Picchu.

The following morning dawned gray and drizzly. Arteaga, the innkeeper, had to be coaxed with a Peruvian silver dollar before he would act as guide. Bingham's friends, not inclined to go mountain climbing in such weather, were left to their own devices. Bingham, Arteaga, and the police sergeant went it alone. They walked up the Urubamba River for nearly an hour, then crossed its roaring rapids on a precarious Indian bridge made of splintered logs and vines. "I am frank to confess," Bingham would write later, "that I got down on my hands and knees and crawled across, six inches at a time."*

Leaving the Urubamba, the three men plunged into the jungle and soon reached the base of a rocky slope. On all fours, they climbed until noon in the oppressive heat. Part of the way up there were only vines to help them over the slippery face of the

* Hiram Bingham, *Lost City of the Incas* (New York: Atheneum, 1963), p. 149.

rain-washed rock. And througout their climb they worried about snakes: the venomous fer-de-lance infested the region.

At 2,000 feet, they met several good-natured Indians who, surprised but delighted to have unexpected company, provided a feast of cool water and sweet potatoes. Two Quechua farmers, Richarte and Alvarez, had chosen this isolated precipice for their home. Here, they explained cheerfully, they were free from the grasp of government tax collectors and out of the reach of army officials seeking "recruits." They grew their crops on agricultural terraces built four centuries ago by Inca workers.

Arteaga lingered on to gossip with the natives, but a small boy was dispatched to lead Bingham to the ruins. At the top of the mountain promontory, the young American scholar found what he had been looking for.

At first, he saw only a single flight of aged stone stairs. Then his eyes began to distinguish under the choking vegetation the outlines of granite walls, buildings, and plazas. Machu Picchu, never reached by the invading Spanish, was a secret no longer.

Quickly, Bingham returned to Yale to organize a new expedition to clear and investigate the entire site. It was not until he returned the following year that he realized the full extent of his discovery—or the difficulties involved in retrieving it.

The first order of business was to build a new bridge across the Urubamba (the bridge so cautiously crossed by Bingham on his first visit to Machu Picchu tumbled into the rapids a few days later) and an improved trail up to the mountain saddle to permit the transportation of supplies and equipment. Despite delays, reluctant Indian labor, poisonous snakes, and raging grass fires, these tasks were accomplished. Engineers moved in to clear the ghostly ruins, a job that continued throughout most of 1912; every two or three months, workers had to go back and clear away plants that re-established themselves with amazing rapidity.

Meanwhile, Bingham had his own problems. Although wages offered at Machu Picchu were high compared with those paid by nearby plantations, the Quechua Indians had been so exploited in the past that they were reluctant to leave their own villages to work at the excavation site. Bingham had brought a few reliable workers with him from Cuzco. For the rest of his labor force, he depended on village officials who, under orders from the Peruvian government, supplied occasional work crews. Many of these stayed only a few days, collected their wages, and disappeared, never to be seen again.

Bingham resorted to bribery in an attempt to retain an adequate work force at the site. Each morning he passed out coca leaves, chewed by the natives for their mild intoxicating effect. He also took to giving workers small gifts on payday; mirrors were in great demand and were enthusiastically accepted. Nevertheless, Bingham never knew how many laborers would show up on any given day. Sometimes there were forty or more; at times he worked with only nine or ten men.

He was also annoyed with the new Peruvian government that came into power during the course of excavations. The old government, under President Augusto Leguía, expressed keen interest in the work at Machu Picchu and lent every possible aid. In painful contrast, officials of the new regime bombarded Bingham with wordy decrees reminding him that he must not injure or deface the ruins in any way. Bingham was peeved: not only had he taken great pains to preserve the beauty of the buildings at Machu Picchu, but he had spent two full days erasing charcoal graffiti scrawled on the walls by the first Peruvian visitors to the site!

Despite frequent delays and labor difficulties, work progressed. Crews of machete-wielding natives attacked the hardwood forest that had grown up on city terraces and on top of many of the buildings, then burned or carted away the debris. Engineers traced and restored walls and roads. Bingham himself worked at scraping centuries of accumulated moss and mold from rock walls. Gradually the jungle receded; the ancient Inca "city in the clouds" began to emerge in magnificent detail.

More than 100 stone stairways—with more than 3,000 steps—course through this multilevel outpost. Some have but 3 or 4 steps, others as many as 150. In several places, an entire flight of 6 to 10 steps was carved from a single massive block of granite. One stairway, apparently used as the main street, leads from the lowest levels to the city's summit; it is bisected along the way by narrow paths that descend through a labyrinth of passageways. At Machu

Plate 1. Entrance to Machu Picchu. *(Photo courtesy Prudential-Grace Lines)*

Plate 2. Machu Picchu and surrounding peaks: panoramic view. *(Photo courtesy Prudential-Grace Lines)*

Plate 3. Machu Picchu: ruined dwellings and garden terraces. *(Photo courtesy Prudential-Grace Lines)*

Picchu, where an entire village perched on the side of a mountain, space was at a premium. Houses were clustered close together, interconnected by tiny residential garden plots and ingeniously designed stairways, some so narrow that only a child could pass along them and some so steep that they had to be climbed like ladders. Whenever possible, steps and passageways were built to follow the natural declivity of the terrain.

Several mountain springs bubble to the surface within a mile of the city proper. From these, the Incas built narrow stone *azequias,* or conduits, which entered the city near its highest point. Fresh water cascaded down through the town via a network of aqueducts, baths, and fountains. Along the length of the main stairway, a series of catch basins trapped water from the central aqueduct. Villagers must have gathered here to wash and to fill their earthenware jugs. Overflow spilled into a duct carved into the stone below and was carried down to the next level.

Engineers still marvel over Machu Picchu's complex aqueduct system. But perhaps the most striking feature at the site is the stonework itself. The Incas had no iron tools, no cranes or derricks to help them lift and adjust the massive blocks of granite with which they erected their walls. Using crude bronze implements—simple chisels and crowbars—they managed nevertheless to become the most masterful stonemasons known in history.

Their craftsmanship reached a peak at Machu Picchu. Here walls were constructed of gigantic granite blocks cut and fitted so closely together that no mortar was needed—and not even the blade of a knife can be inserted between the joints today.

Many of the blocks used in building weigh more than a ton. And no two are alike: Each was cut with unique angles and protuberances to suit its particular position in the architectural whole. One extraordinary example, found in the structure known as the Priest's House, boasts thirty-two angles!

Because building stones were keyed, hooking firmly into one another, the buildings at Machu Picchu have withstood earthquakes, settling, and torrential rains for more than four centuries —while at nearby Cuzco more-recent Spanish dwellings have been toppled by the destructive action of time and weather.

Several groups of dwellings at Machu Picchu, possibly intended

Plate 4. Machu Picchu: wall and watchtower, showing Inca construction. *(Photo courtesy Organization of American States)*

for the sons or daughters of nobility, appear to have been constructed with special care. Their walls stand today in a state of near-perfect preservation.

But perhaps the finest workmanship is found in the Principal Temple, a structure that was left entirely open to the Sacred Plaza on the south and that was enclosed on the other three sides by 12-foot stone walls. The temple is dominated by an immense granite altar, probably designed to receive the mummies of honored dead. Above the altar, the Incas carved numerous small niches for food or other funeral offerings.

It is likely that it was to this elaborately designed structure that the inhabitants of Machu Picchu carried the mummies of their dead. Bingham believes that the temple never had a roof. "If it were the place in which the mummies of departed ancestors were brought for the purposes of worship," he wrote, "the presence of a roof would have been undesirable and would have interfered with the ceremony of giving the mummies a comfortable sun bath."*

It is not so outlandish a suggestion as it seems. In ancient Peru, the dead were treated as if they were alive. Honored mummies were frequently brought out, re-dressed, and advised of current events. No efforts were spared to ensure their comfort.

Across the Sacred Plaza is located the Temple of the Three Windows, which offers a panoramic view of the surrounding countryside and of the rising sun. For Bingham, this structure seemed to fit the description of the legendary royal house from which the first Inca set forth to establish his empire—although, in fact, Bingham's temple boasts not just three but five windows.

But it is the *Intihuantana,* or Sundial Stone, that crowns this isolated mountain citadel. The Incas were sun-worshipers; in each of their cities a sacred sundial served to mark the course of the sun and hence played a significant role in Inca ceremonial life. For the Incas, the short days and long shadows of winter brought a fear that the sun might one day go too far, losing its way in the vastness of the universe. And so they erected, in each Inca town, an *Intihuantana* to represent the post to which they ceremoniously tied the sun, preventing it from straying. At Machu Picchu, the *Intihuantana* is located at the very top of a small hill near the highest point of the city; below, clustered ruins jut skyward, as if to underscore the importance of the sacred sundial.

While a crew of workmen labored to clear vegetation and rocky debris from these ancient structures, Bingham searched for burial caves. The Quechua Indians Richarte and Alvarez were sent to explore the wooded slopes outside the city proper, but returned empty-handed. Finally, Bingham promised a Peruvian silver dollar to anyone who found a cave containing human bones. But he wisely stipulated that the cave must be left exactly as it was found, with the bones in position and undisturbed.

Richarte and Alvarez ambled quietly away, while the other natives plunged headlong into the jungle on a feverish hunt for Inca burials. One by one, they returned to camp, scratched and torn by the thorny scrub and bamboo vines that encircled the

* Ibid., p. 179.

Plate 5. Machu Picchu: *Intihuantana,* or Sundial Stone.
(Photo courtesy Prudential-Grace Lines)

city; one had split his big toe with a machete in his haste to hew his way through the dense thicket. Richarte and Alvarez, on the other hand, returned at day's end with beaming faces and untorn clothing, announcing that they had discovered *eight* burial caves and would like to receive their bonus of eight dollars.

"These," wrote Bingham later in exasperation, "were the same Indians who had found 'nothing' on the two preceding days." Apparently, the Quechuas had known of the existence of Inca burials in the vicinity but were unwilling to reveal their locations until a suitable prize was offered.

Before the season's end, Bingham's party had opened more than 100 burial caves, retrieving the bones of 173 individuals. At least 150 of them appeared to be female.

Was Machu Picchu a city of women? Bingham thought it was, at least in its final stages. It was the custom in pre-Columbian Peru for the Inca government to maintain in Cuzco and in other provincial capitals special schools for the training of *Ñustas,* or Chosen Women. The most beautiful and talented young women in the Inca Empire were selected and called to these schools to learn the techniques of weaving, cooking, and featherwork. Some would eventually serve in the household of the Inca king, holding his plate as he dined or fashioning the brilliant feathered tunics he wore on ceremonial occasions. Others, instructed in religious rituals and called Handmaidens of the Sun, served in the all-important sun-worship ceremonies.

Bingham believed that Machu Picchu was the cradle of Inca civilization, that it was from here that Manco Capac, the first Inca king, emerged to establish his capital at Cuzco around A.D. 1200. Centuries later, when the Spanish invaded Peru and the empire began to topple, a retinue of Chosen Women fled secretly to Machu Picchu, seeking sanctuary. Here they might live in safety and seclusion, devoting their lives to the time-honored worship of the Inca sun-god until the Spanish were repelled.

The Incas, of course, never regained power. Tupac Amaru, last of the royal line, was assassinated by the Spaniards in 1572, and the reign of the aristocratic Incas was ended. Machu Picchu, its location never revealed, was forgotten.

Modern authorities dispute Bingham's claim that Machu Picchu was the birthplace of the first Inca king. Its architecture is typical of the late Inca period, and experts are generally agreed that this remarkable mountain outpost was less than a century old at the time of the Spanish Conquest. Beyond this single fact, present-day authorities find little ground for agreement. Controversy rages over the city's true origin and history.

Why did the Incas choose this remote, inaccessible location? How did they span the perilous Urubamba to reach the twin peaks of Machu Picchu and Huayna Picchu? How did they construct this city, with primitive tools and at a dizzying height? And why did they flee, leaving their stately temples to be overgrown by the surrounding jungle?

We may never know the answers, but theories abound. Some say that Machu Picchu was a fortified mountain stronghold built at the direction of Viracocha, eighth in the Inca Dynasty, for defense against enemy Indians. Certainly the city, poised on a narrow ridge deep within a stupendous granite canyon, is extraordinarily defensible. It is flanked by tremendous cliffs, some more than 1,000 feet sheer, and surrounded on three sides by the rapids of the mighty Urubamba. To the north of the city, paths along the razor-sharp ridges of the mountain saddle are so narrow they could be defended by as few as two men. To the south, inner and outer walls afforded additional protection. There was but a single city gate, which could be secured by a powerful crossbar. A handful of determined warriors might hold the city almost indefinitely against an army of vigorous attackers.

Yet there is more to Machu Picchu than fortifications. There were barracks, to be sure. But there were temples, plazas, jails, cemeteries, and residential buildings as well. Certain structures were clearly designed as centers for religious and governmental activities. The dwellings differ in size and quality of construction, indicating that the inhabitants of Machu Picchu were differentiated according to social class and occupation. Agricultural terraces surrounding the town provided a year-round supply of foodstuffs adequate to support a permanent population of from 1,000 to 8,000 people. And water was conveniently piped in to supply public baths and fountains. Obviously, the elements of a true city are present in this remote Inca settlement. Whatever the original function of Machu Picchu, the city served in its prime as more than a military outpost.

Some think that it was Pachacuti, son of Viracocha, who founded the city on Machu Picchu Mountain. It was Pachacuti, crowned about A.D. 1438, who began to consolidate territorial gains and thus initiated the major expansion of the Inca Empire.

In earlier eras, the typical pattern of Inca warfare was strike-and-run. Beginning with the reign of Pachacuti, the Incas began to occupy conquered lands, exacting "labor taxes" from original inhabitants in order to obtain manpower for tending agricultural terraces and building roads. The Incas were not popular among the peoples they conquered—and they knew it. It was their practice to erect strong defenses—much like those found at Machu Picchu—against their reluctant hosts, who remained outside city walls except when needed inside as laborers.

Some suggest that Machu Picchu was no more than a mountain resort built and maintained for the pleasure of the Inca nobility. The Incas were inordinately fond of scenic views; and if they were to choose a vacation paradise, it might well have been here. From a citadel perched on the side of Machu Picchu Mountain, the sons and daughters of royalty might enjoy a dazzling panorama of snow-capped peaks and clouds; the roaring Urubamba was a silvery ribbon below. But there is no evidence to suggest that the town was occupied on a seasonal basis, nor that the Inca king maintained a vacation retreat.

Others say that Machu Picchu must have been designed to serve as a secret convent, housing a specially selected covey of Chosen Women. Here, guarded by soldiers and protected from the prying eyes of outsiders, the *Ñustas* might learn the sacred rituals of Inca sun worship or train for service in the royal household. But this also is speculation. Usually, Inca schools for the education of the sun god's Chosen Women were located in the larger provincial capitals. And Machu Picchu, however elaborate, was a small Inca settlement.

For Bingham, the city on Machu Picchu Mountain represented the culmination of "generations if not centuries of effort." And without doubt, back-breaking toil must have gone into the construction of this complex little citadel. Yet modern investigators insist that the city could not have been built before the reign of Pachacuti and that it must have been abandoned shortly after the time of the Spanish Conquest. Of course, this means that Machu Picchu had a total life span of no more than sixty years, give or take a single decade. It is an amazingly brief occupation for so elaborate a city.

How did the Incas erect so complex an outpost in this short span of time? They lacked both wheel and heavy pack animals. And yet they moved massive granite blocks from quarries more than a mile from the city and arranged them into buildings so skillfully that the ruins seem almost impervious.

And why did the Incas abandon their jewel-like city in the clouds? Bingham believed that a dwindling water supply might account for the sudden desertion. Mountain springs may have been insufficient to meet the demands of a growing population. Yet those same mountain springs supply water for the thousands of tourists who now visit Machu Picchu each year.

A few archaeologists offer a simpler explanation for the city's prehistoric demise. Although the Incas enjoyed scenic views, they disliked hot, humid weather. Perhaps the temperatures of the tropical region in which Machu Picchu is located became intolerable, and the Incas left when they had the chance to move to the cooler highland regions of Peru. For other archaeologists, this is a flimsy, superficial theory. Why would the Incas build here in the first place if the climate was not to their liking?

Perhaps Machu Picchu was, after all, a final refuge for people who saw their vast empire crumbling under the weight of internal disruptions, imported disease, and superior foreign forces. Built before the Spanish Conquest and surrounded by both natural and man-made fortifications, the hidden city may have provided an ideal sanctuary for priests, Chosen Women, and escort-warriors who fled the disaster that descended upon Cuzco with the coming of Pizarro's troops.

We may never know the answer. It may be that the key to the mystery of Machu Picchu will be found someday in one of the 50,000 yet unexplored Inca sites scattered throughout the region.

Machu Picchu was just one of a network of fortress cities; perhaps clue's to its purpose and destiny will be unearthed in the rubble of a sister citadel.

Until more clues are brought to light, we can only speculate about this granite city in the clouds.

3

The Riddle of the Trepanned Skulls

Not only ruins and relics but also human bones make up the debris of past life so diligently probed by archaeologists. And in the bony remains, there are also mysteries to ponder.

For more than a century, scientists have puzzled over strangely incised human skulls recovered from dozens of archaeological sites around the world. The most specimens come from ancient tombs in Bolivia and Peru. They provide startling evidence that here Stone Age skull surgery was both commonplace and successful.

The first of these skulls came to light sometime between 1863 and 1865, when the American diplomat-anthropologist E. G. Squier traveled to Cuzco, Peru, in search of native antiquities. While browsing through a private archaeological collection, Squier came upon a portion of a human skull from which a huge rectangular section of bone had been removed. Intrigued, Squier purchased the skull and quickly dispatched it to France for analy-

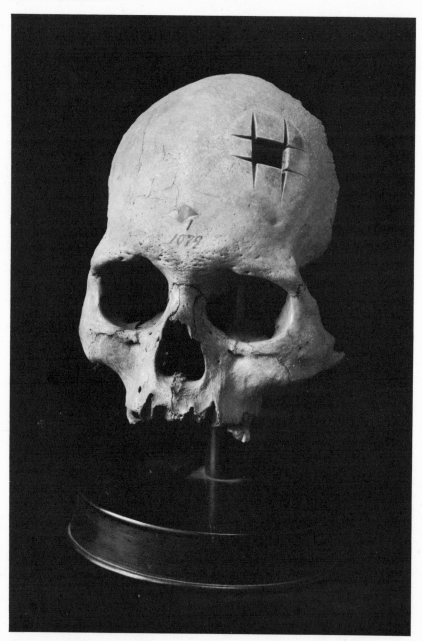

Plate 6. Squier's "Inca skull," from Yucay, Peru. *(Photo courtesy the American Museum of Natural History)*

sis by Paul Broca, a prominent medically trained anthropologist.

Broca was an old hand at identifying osteological specimens, and he immediately recognized the skull as that of a pre-Columbian Indian from South America. But the artificial opening, cut into the skull by means of four neat incisions arranged in a tictactoe pattern, fascinated him: he had never before viewed such prehistoric handiwork.

What he *had* noted, in his previous European excavations, was an abundance of amulets, or charms, fashioned from small bits of human skull bone. It is a common belief among many primitive peoples that great magic dwells in the head of a fallen enemy and that the living can capture the magic for their own uses by preserving head or skull parts. Trepanation—the surgical removal of portions of the human skull—seemed to Broca a likely source of bone in ancient times. He theorized that prehistoric man in Europe operated on the skull after death to obtain rondels of bone for use in making charms and talismans—objects designed to ward off evil spirits or bring strength and good fortune through their magical properties. Obviously, Squier's Peruvian skull was no more than a New World example of prehistoric trepanation performed for magicoreligious purposes.

Or was it? In the "Inca skull" Broca found something new and totally unexpected: unmistakable evidence of infection in the bone surrounding the cuts. Apparently, this trepanation had been performed not after death but during life—and the patient had survived the operation for at least seven to fifteen days, long enough for infection to leave its marks on the bone.

It was a controversial idea, and one that would be hotly debated. But since Broca's original diagnosis, a century of excavation and analysis has brought to light hundreds of examples of prehistoric trepanation from sites in Europe, Asia, Africa, North and South America, and the Pacific. Many bear evidence of patient survival. The earliest specimen recovered so far comes from Cannstadt, near Stuttgart, West Germany, and dates from 3000 B.C.—an astonishingly early time for man to have dabbled in cranial surgery.

Trepanation, performed today under rigorously controlled and antiseptic conditions, remains a dramatic test of a trained sur-

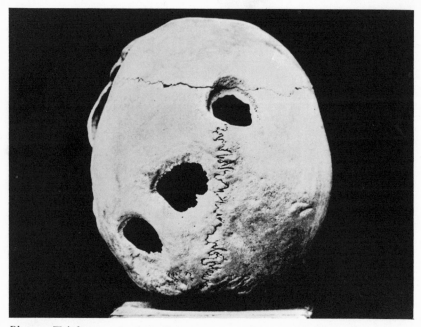

Plate 7. Triple-trepanned skull from Cuzco. *(Photo courtesy Bureau of American Ethnology)*

geon's skill. And yet, remarkable as are our modern achievements in brain surgery, the skeletal evidence indicates that prehistoric man attempted skull surgery in a primitive and unsanitary environment and did so with extraordinary success.

Despite the risk of fatal hemorrhage, the ever-present danger of severe bacterial infection, and the brutal nature of the operation itself, a majority of prehistoric South American trepanation patients survived their ordeals. Many submitted to second or third treatments (Plate 7). A few mutilated skulls from Peru bear the healed scars of as many as *five* subsequent operations!

In most trepanned skulls, experts find it relatively easy to distinguish between post-mortem and ante-mortem surgeries. Healing is evidenced by new bone growth at the site of the wound or by increased porosity of the bone adjacent to the cut—conditions never encountered when the operation was performed on a corpse for the purpose of obtaining bone discs. If the healing process is apparent, authorities must conclude that a living human being submitted to the knife—and lived to tell of his experience. Scientists find advanced stages of healing in from 55 to 63 per cent of the trepanned Peruvian skulls examined. Other estimates, based on the analysis of skulls less reliably documented, range as high as 80 per cent.

Who were the people who risked this radical, dangerous surgery —and toward what mysterious ends? Archaeologists have recovered no fewer than 370 trepanned skulls from prehistoric Europe alone, and these range in time from 3000 to 200 B.C. It is in Europe, as Broca noted, that bone amulets frequently appear in ancient graves. Apparently, ancient Europeans invented trepanation as a means of acquiring the materials needed for making magical charms. Later, they may have performed the operation on living captives.

In Asia, trepanned skulls have been found at Dagestan, west of the Caspian Sea, and in a single large Palestinian cemetery dating from the seventh century B.C. Here natives not only cut into the living skull but also cauterized the scalp with boiling oils and resins in the belief that this drastic measure might prevent future illnesses.

In Algeria, mutilated skulls appear in sites dating from Roman times. But no evidence survives to hint at the motives for the surgery here, and trepanation seems to have occurred only rarely elsewhere in Africa.

Trepanned skulls have been found at scattered sites throughout the Pacific. Hair-raising examples come from New Zealand, the Marquesas, and the Tuamotu archipelago. Records of early European expeditions into Pacific waters tell us that trepanation was a practice common on the island of Samoa until the latter part of the nineteenth century. Here the surgery was accomplished by scraping the skull with crude flint knives. After the Samoans had made contact with Europeans, bits of broken glass were used. Carefully prepared pieces of coconut shell, fitted into the openings left by the surgeon's blade, protected the brain from postoperative damage.

When questioned, natives defended the operation on medical grounds. Trepanning, they insisted, was a quick and certain cure for the discomfort of headache, neuralgia, or vertigo. Anthropologists suspect that the underlying motive was magical rather than medical, that the operation was designed to release evil spirits that, lurking inside the victim's body, caused pain, emotional suffering, and erratic behavior.

Anthropologists are aware that surgery is mixed with magic throughout the primitive world as a form of exorcism. Trepanation, like bloodletting, was believed to release malevolent spirits. Possession by such spirits was a dread condition considered everywhere in early times to result in intolerable pain and suffering, if not in death itself. For believers, almost any dramatic symptom —dizziness, coma, convulsion, epileptic seizure, or vision-blurring headache—seemed indicative of spiritual possession.

Disease and injury have no rival, even today, as man's greatest enemies. But in a primitive world where the slightest indisposition threatens a man's survival, it is no wonder that man attempts the most drastic of healing measures. He is by nature a mystic. And his is a world filled with psychic dangers.

Of all ancient trepanners, none were so experienced or so skilled as the Indians of pre-Columbian Peru. It was here that the art of trepanation found its most remarkable expression. More trepanned skulls have been collected from sites in Peru than in all other world regions combined. Museum specimens alone number well over one thousand and make Peru the surgical capital of the prehistoric world.

The earliest mutilated skulls so far recovered in the New World come from Paracas, in southern Peru, where archaeologists have unearthed hundreds of perfectly preserved mummies more than two thousand years old. Of the incised skulls found among them, only a tiny fraction bear marks of healing; apparently, the most ancient of American surgeons had not mastered the delicate techniques of trepanation.

Or was it that the Indians of Paracas cut into the living skull with more sinister motives? Head-hunting is not uncommon among the untamed tribes of South America. Even today, the Jivaro Indians who roam the jungles of the Amazon are feared for their custom of shrinking and preserving the heads of slain enemies. Smithsonian Institution anthropologist T. Dale Stewart, noting the fresh-cut appearance of incisions in skulls from Paracas, suggests that these specimens might represent the remnants of a prehistoric skull cult—a native religion based on the gathering of human-head trophies.

The answer is lost, or not yet found. Certainly later inhabitants of Bolivia and Peru were not head-hunters. And their tombs are littered with incised skulls that bear the unmistakable marks of postoperative healing. These specimens, boasting as they do clear signs of healthy new bone growth following trepanation, provide tantalizing proof of surgeries in which patient recovery was the primary goal—and the usual result as well.

Few objects of antiquity so captivate the modern imagination as do these skulls from Peru. For these remains conjure up, even in the most scholarly mind, vivid images of primitive magic and medicine. Many archaeologists, having traveled to Peru to examine cultural artifacts or reconstructed native cities, find themselves poring instead over trepanned skulls. Physicians and physical anthropologists return again and again to museum collections, hoping to find that one elusive clue that will explain the spectacular success with which the ancient Peruvians cut into the living skull.

First to attempt a full-scale investigation of trepanning in prehistoric Peru were Manuel Antonio Muniz, a Peruvian surgeon, and W. J. McGee, a self-trained anthropologist. As Surgeon-General of the army of Peru, Muniz had traveled extensively throughout the former realm of the Incas. Wherever he went, he explored ancient graves and tombs, and eventually he amassed an enviable collection of artifacts, mummies, and bones. Although Dr. Muniz gathered an assortment of cultural relics including tools, weapons, domestic utensils, and jewelry, his interest and training led him to focus his attention on the human skeletal remains he had recovered. Among these were nineteen well-preserved incised skulls. All were unquestionable examples of trepanning, and all came from burials that predated Columbus by more than two hundred years.

In 1893, Dr. Muniz left Peru to exhibit the skulls at the International Congress of Anthropology in Chicago and to attend the Pan-American Medical Congress in Washington, D.C. Fortunately, he chose to leave the cranial collection there, in the custody of the Bureau of American Ethnology, for he encountered, on his return to Lima, a chaotic political movement that drove him into exile. His home was sacked and burned, his library destroyed, his archaeological treasures plundered. Of the rich collections so arduously gathered during years of exploring, only the skulls left in Washington remained.

The Muniz crania were photographed, analyzed, and described by W. J. McGee in a monograph published by the Smithsonian Institution in 1897. McGee, who lacked medical training, over-looked subtle signs of healing in several of the Muniz skulls. He regarded the Peruvian practice of trepanning as an aimless oper-ation designed by ill-informed primitives to supplement their magical cures. The Peruvian trepanations, he wrote, were "ill-planned, clumsy, and extravagent." To Julio Tello, a Peruvian Indian who had both medical and anthropological training—and for other experts who consider the Peruvian trepannings to be the boldest and most remarkable of all early surgical procedures—those were uninformed words.

Tello first became intrigued with the ancient inhabitants of his country as a child, when his older brother was hired to collect skulls for Dr. Muniz. Later, while pursuing his medical studies at San Marcos in Lima, Tello came across the McGee report. His interest once more aroused, Tello switched from medicine to anthropology, taking a master's degree at Harvard. In time, he was ready to challenge McGee's evaluation of surgical skill in pre-historic Peru.

Tello assembled a new collection of trepanned skulls and drew on his medical training to detect subtle changes in the bone that indicate postoperative healing and patient recovery. When he finished, he was convinced that the early surgeries were neither clumsy nor ill planned but provided undeniable proof of surgical skill at a remarkably early date.

According to Tello, all cases of Peruvian trepanation could be explained on therapeutic grounds; that is, the Indians of ancient Peru cut into the living skull not with some crude notion of re-leasing evil spirits but as a deliberate and practical means of al-leviating pain caused by cuts, fractures, and other head injuries. And they did so with astonishing success: Of the skulls collected and analyzed by Tello in his initial study, a sizable majority showed unmistakable signs of patient recovery.

Later investigations in Peru tend to support Tello's hypothesis. Numerous trepanned skulls exhibit not only the surgical incisions but also the scars of cranial fracture. And, although women and children submitted to the operation, the vast majority of trepanation patients were adult males, perhaps representatives of a warrior class. At Machu Picchu, where most of the skeletons taken from burial caves and cemeteries are those of women and children, not a single trepanned skull has come to light. And yet hundreds of examples come from sites within 25 miles of that mysterious mountain citadel.

Further, in the regions where archaeologists find great numbers of trepanned skulls, they find also the fierce star-shaped maces peculiar to Peruvian warfare. These vicious instruments, designed to be hurled from slingshots at the head of an advancing enemy, caused agonizing head wounds. They are largely responsible for the high incidence of skull fracture noted among Peruvian skeletal remains.

It seems possible that the people who wielded such weapons would devise a means of treating injuries caused by them. If so, trepanation is the cure they settled upon.

But even if it is true that trepanning was a therapeutic measure intended to combat the effects of head injury, how do we account for the fact that so many people were willing, under such dangerous conditions, to risk this extraordinary surgery? A few anthropologists, reluctant to accept the startling suggestion that prehistoric man could survive Stone Age skull surgery, continue to insist that the operation was performed only upon the dead, as in Europe, for the purpose of obtaining bone discs.

But no amulets made from human skull bone have ever been found among the archaeological remains of Peru. Moreover, bone sections removed from most of the trepanned skulls are too small to have been used to manufacture magical charms. And evidence of healing—and hence of patient survival and recovery—cannot be ignored.

Scientists who have studied the ancient cultures of South America contend that post-mortem surgery is not consistent with the

Peruvian way of life. Among the Incas, dead rulers and honored noblemen were mummified and treated as living beings. Mummies were entitled to servants, regular meals, and daily visits from living relatives. They retained both their wealth, accumulated during life, and their interest in household matters. And they were accorded the utmost respect. The Peruvian veneration of the dead never would have permitted the desecration of the head or body after death. Most anthropologists agree that trepanation, at least in Peru, was reserved for the living.

How did primitive Indian surgeons accomplish this daring surgery? Ancient pottery jars decorated with representations of surgical scenes confirm the fact of trepanation but shed little light on actual procedures. The cuts and scars on trepanned skulls are a bit more enlightening. And, in perhaps the boldest of experiments in "living prehistory," at least two modern Peruvian sur-

Figure 2. Types of trepan holes: *A,* by drilling holes and cutting through the divisions between; *B,* by slowly cutting out a roundel with metal or flint tool; *C,* by four incisions that enclose a rectangular area of bone. *(Reproduced by courtesy of D. R. Brothwell and the British Museum [Natural History])*

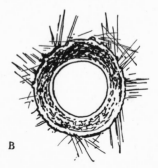

A

B

C

geons have operated on living heads with tools and implements retrieved from ancient graves.

Prehistoric Peruvians cut into the skull with stone tools, usually sharp-edged blades chipped from blocks of flint or obsidian. Bits of shell and animal bone were used for scraping and smoothing roughened edges of the wound.

First the scalp was incised and peeled back to expose the brain case. Then an opening was made in one of several ways (Figure 2). If a round hole was desired, the surgeon cut and scraped in a circular fashion until he had produced an opening with a neat beveled edge. Or he drilled a series of small holes in a circular pattern and later severed the slender connections between them. Some early surgeons favored a rectangular opening produced by four canoe-shaped cuts, as in Squier's famous "Inca skull."

Stone or wooden probes were used to pry away loose bone sections or other fragments. Often, the opening was covered with discs of shell or pounded metal. In one mummy from Paracas, a thin gold plate had been carefully fitted over the trepan hole.

No evidence survives to tell of prehistoric anesthesia. But most primitive peoples had a stockpile of herbal drugs that could be turned to use as sedatives or narcotics. It is only reasonable to assume that a person contemplating this surgical ordeal would have availed himself of any sleep-inducing potion known to him. Trepanation must indeed have been painful: On many of the mutilated skulls, huge hacking cuts mar the bone surface near the opening (Plate 8). These gashes were exploratory, made as the surgeon set to his task. They provide graphic evidence of the dangers of the operation.

And yet patients survived in great number, often returning for subsequent operations. And this is the mystery that remains. Over a century of investigations, scientists have succeeded in discovering the motives and reconstructing many of the methods involved in this most daring kind of prehistoric surgery. But they have not yet accounted for the remarkable rate of recovery enjoyed among the trepanation patients in pre-Columbian Peru.

Postoperative dressings, it is true, may have been applied to combat infection. In many skulls, investigators note a bone inflammation called osteitis, a condition probably arising from the

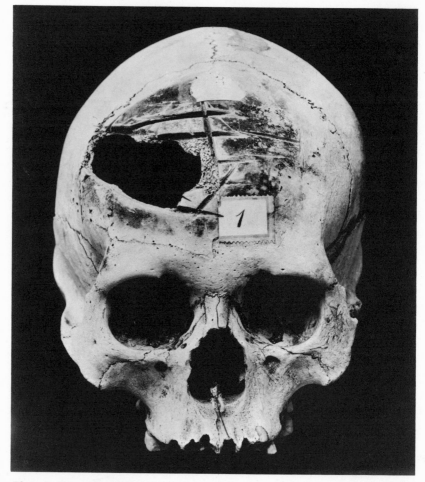

Plate 8. Trepanned skull from Huarochiri, Peru. *(Photo courtesy Smithsonian Institution)*

application of boiling oils or resins. But boiling oils could not have circumvented the danger of fatal hemorrhage or protected against the rigors of shock to the patient's nervous system.

Perhaps we overdramatize the courage and fortitude of these patients. The awe one feels at the sight of ancient mutilated skulls is largely conditioned by one's awareness of the importance of the living brain. Prehistoric man was not bothered by such sophisticated knowledge. Ignorant—by our standards—of human physiology, he may have approached trepanation with serene confidence, devoid of the uncertainty we exhibit in the face of cranial surgery.

But psychological factors alone cannot explain the spectacular success with which primitive Peruvian Indians cut deep into the living brain case. What factors stemmed the tide of fatal hemorrhage? What forces guarded against shock and bacterial infection?

We know only that the trepanned skulls from Peru provide stark evidence of prehistoric man's will to sustain life. We have surpassed his medical achievements. But we may never know the secrets of his surgical success.

The Mysterious Nazca Markings

For those who investigate the American past, few pre-Columbian peoples are so intriguing as those of Inca Peru. The Incas had no wheeled vehicles. Their knowledge of animal domestication was severely limited. For beasts of burden, they had only the llama and alpaca, suitable for relatively light loads. They domesticated only the guinea pig for food. As far as we know, they lacked even a rudimentary written language.

And yet they established what was perhaps the most sophisticated and well-organized government in all the New World. The vast Inca Empire, ruled by a living god, stretched along the Andes for more than 2,500 miles, ranging from the southernmost boundaries of Colombia to the Maule River in central Chile. Armies of workers, using tools of stone and bronze, accomplished feats of engineering unsurpassed even today. Trained relay runners formed a human communications network, linking the Inca capital with its far-flung outposts. Irrigation canals and agricultural terraces brought millions of acres of land into active production.

Some of these canals and terraces are in use today, after a span of four centuries. Many of the well-built Inca roads, although too narrow for use by modern jeeps or automobiles, are traveled with ease and frequency by the present-day inhabitants of the region. Beneath the rubble of Spanish colonial structures toppled by earthquakes rest the undamaged foundations of Inca walls and dwellings. And from the tombs of pre-Columbian Peru come perfectly preserved Inca mummies wrapped in fine, bright-colored textiles that have withstood the ravages of time. To gaze upon such remnants of the Inca Empire is to arrest time, capturing brief glimpses into a romantic past. Little wonder, then, that this great native empire holds such fascination for those who probe American prehistory.

The Inca civilization represented the culmination of thousands of years of cultural and intellectual development in Peru. The Incas were comparative late-comers, rising to power less than a century before the Spanish Conquest. They were preceded by diverse fragmented Indian tribes whose complex histories are lost in time. Among these early inhabitants of Peru were little-known desert peoples who raised remarkably high cultures centuries before the birth of the first Inca king.

To the west of the Andes is a barren, inhospitable desert that runs some 2,000 miles along the coast of Peru. This is a region of intense heat. Much of the desert is totally devoid of life. And to the modern visitor, it seems incredible that man could wrest a living from this harsh environment.

Fog occasionally crowds in from the coastal waters, but rain never falls here. There are, however, small rivers and streams that carry water to the sea from the forested slopes of the Andes, where rains are torrential. Through tedious and painstaking techniques of irrigation, crops can be grown here. And where food can be grown, people can survive.

In the northern range of the coastal desert lived a hardy, warlike people known as the Mochicas. About A.D. 200, Mochica peoples formed a loose confederacy of groups living in adjoining valleys. Our knowledge of their culture comes primarily from the pottery they buried with their dead.

The Mochicas were skilled sculptors, modeling in clay the forms they had seen or fantasied. Among the modeled pottery recovered from desert excavations in northern Peru are vessels shaped like fish, owls, deer, monkeys, birds, frogs, and fierce, fanged gods. There are human forms, too, and clay portraits so masterfully executed that they are startling in their realism. Not only the usual but also the bizarre caught the attention of Mochica sculptors. The pottery they left behind includes grotesque representations of disease and physical deformity—and graphic portrayals of human sexual activity. Ancient Mochica pottery is abundant in modern collections of pornographic art.

Painted vessels give us heady glimpses into the daily lives of the Mochicas. On their smooth, brightly colored surfaces are represented people from all walks of Mochica life. There are chiefs, merchants, craftsmen, mothers, warriors, hunters, weavers, and musicians—all dressed in suitable costume and engaged in appropriate activity.

Near the center of Peru's coastal desert, predating Mochica culture by nearly two centuries, flourished another unique Indian race. They were the Paracas, known primarily for their extraordinary textiles and exquisite embroidered garments. Miraculously preserved by the arid desert air, these are as vivid today as they were when first woven. Like the Incas to come later, the Paracas venerated their dead. The mummies of chiefs, priests, and honored noblemen were wrapped first in plain cotton shrouds, then enveloped in yards of fine, beautifully woven fabric; tucked deep within the mummy wrappings were offerings of food and gold. Archaeologists have recovered several hundred Paracas mummies. At one site alone—Paracas Necropolis—excavators unearthed more than four hundred seated mummies, all elaborately prepared and preserved for posterity.

But it is to the south of the Paracas region that we find the remains of the most mysterious of Peru's desert kingdoms. Across the southern coast, about 250 miles from Lima, the Rio Grande River branches out into eight small tributaries. These are dry for more than half the year; nevertheless, there is sufficient water to irrigate the intervening valleys and thus support their small populations of from one thousand to three thousand people.

Between the Nazca and the Ica valleys, from about A.D. 200 to 600, lived an enigmatic Indian race believed to be responsible for the most large scale of all archaeological riddles. In one of the world's driest deserts—and for reasons we may never uncover—the Ica-Nazcas carefully etched into the earth's surface great networks of lines and geometric figures.

Some of the tracings are ruler-straight, running along the desert plains for distances of up to 5 miles; some continue along for no more than a few feet. Others form immense geometric figures— squares, rectangles, trapezoids, triangles—that measure thousands

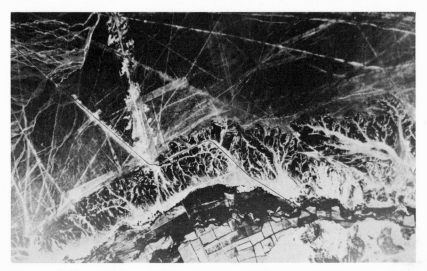

Plate 9. Maze of Nazca markings south of the Ingenio Valley. The sharp black line running across the photograph is the modern Pan American High-way. Note, near middle of photo, a typical "center" from which numerous lines and geometric figures radiate. *(Photo courtesy Servicio, Paul Kosok, and Long Island University Press)*

of feet in width. Still others trace the outlines of birds, plants, monkeys, spiders, and other creatures, or loop round and round in dizzying, seemingly meaningless spirals. One figure, found near a huge trapezoid located close by the Pan-American Highway, consists of a gigantic pair of hands—with but nine fingers.

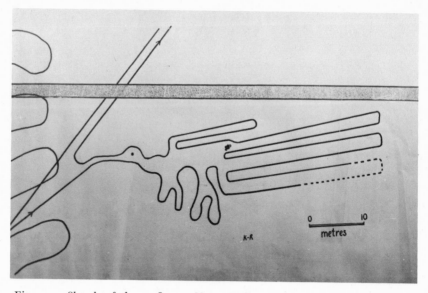

Figure 3. Sketch of desert figure, Nazca Valley. *(Courtesy Long Island University Press)*

Most of the geometric figures are neatly arranged, their borders clearly and concisely outlined. Other lines lace back and forth across the landscape, chaotically overlapping in places, as if they were etched at different times by artists with different interests. There are giant circles, too, and mysterious radiating lines.

The Spanish never mentioned these curious markings in any of their writings. And present-day inhabitants of the region, although aware of the tracings, can shed no light on the mystery. Apparently, the secret of these vast drawings was buried with the people who made them. One Spanish chronicler, Cieza de León, mentions in his writings that all of the Indians of the Nazca Valley died in the civil wars that wreaked havoc on the region as rival Spanish armies battled for possession of New World lands and Indian slaves.

Modern inhabitants of the Nazca Valley as well as tourists who fly over the area refer to the desert etchings as "Inca roads." And, from both air and ground, the majority of the markings look very much like roads, or light-colored trails edged with darker filaments at either border.

Yet the lines predate the Incas by centuries and could not have been used for ordinary purposes of transportation. Most begin and end seemingly nowhere. A true Inca road, built shortly before the Spanish Conquest, runs directly across some of the larger desert figures; the Incas, at least, were totally indifferent to these strange sand drawings.

Both lines and figures appear to have been made by the simple process of removing surface pebbles to expose the lighter soil below. Surface material was then piled along either side of the line. Rocks and gravel on the desert's surface are dark; they contain iron, which becomes oxidized and darkened upon contact with the air—hence the clarity of these prehistoric constructions. A single heavy rainfall would wash away the coat of dust that clings to the rocky outlines of these gigantic forms. But, because it seldom rains in the Nazca Valley, the fragile etchings have survived for centuries.

The Nazca markings are so immense that their true shapes can be ascertained only from the air. Some of the more compex networks cover an area more than 40 miles long and 10 miles wide.

Why did prehistoric peoples labor under the broiling sun to devise these giant figures? How could designs be executed with such precision by peoples who could never view their own handiwork?

When first observed from the air, the Nazca tracings were laughingly called "prehistoric landing strips," and compared to the "canals" on Mars. In 1939, one scholar—Mejia Xesspe—suggested that the desert lines represent ceremonial paths. Eight years later, Professor Hans Horkheimer theorized that the lines might have served, in prehistoric times, to link the graves of members of local families or clans. But no graves have ever been found at the junctures of these connecting lines.

In 1941, an imaginative American historian stumbled upon the most promising clue so far—one that may one day unravel the secret of the mysterious markings. In June of that year, Paul Kosok, then a professor of history at Long Island University in New York, traveled to Peru to study the prehistoric irrigation systems of the northwest coast and their possible relationships with important ruins of the past. With his wife, Dr. Kosok poured over aerial photographs of the region and then decided to explore the so-called Inca roads in the hope that they might represent— or lead to—prehistoric irrigation canals.

Quickly, the Kosoks ruled out the possibility that the tracings had anything to do with irrigation. The lines often ran over small desert hillocks; water in such "canals" would have had to defy the law of gravity. Further, the markings had no physical connection with known rivers, which connection would have been mandatory for any system of irrigation canals.

Even so, the Kosoks continued to explore the region, now thoroughly intrigued by the desert markings. They chose a wide Nazca line that crossed the modern Pan-American Highway to the south of Palpa and followed it on foot as it led straight up one side of a small desert mesa.

There the line came to an abrupt end. But it was surrounded by several similar lines that—together with longer, narrower ones— radiated from a center near which the Kosoks stood.

From this vantage point, Dr. Kosok and his wife commanded a clear view of the horizon and of the surrounding landscape, which was crisscrossed by the huge rectangles and trapezoids typical in the Nazca Valley. They walked to the center of the radiating lines and stood together, watching the setting of the sun.

Then—in one of those rare and wonderful coincidences that sometimes bless one science or another—the sun set almost exactly over the end of one of the long Nazca lines.

A moment later, the Kosoks recalled that the date was June 22, the day of the winter solstice in the Southern Hemisphere—the day when the sun sets farthest north of due west.

Had the peoples of the Nazca Valley etched this line into the desert to mark the winter solstice? If so, did the other strange tracings also represent astronomical events meaningful to the peoples of Peru's coastal desert?

Kosok thought so. As a scholar, he had often contemplated the importance of astronomical observations to regulate the agricultural life of primitive societies across the world. He theorized that the Ica-Nazcas, like other agricultural peoples, must have yearned for an understanding of the productive cycle. In response, they apparently developed numerous calendrical systems—based on astronomical observations—to record the changing seasons and to predict the onset of life-sustaining waters.

Kosok visualized here an ancient Indian society dominated by astronomer-priests who supervised the construction of sight lines intended to mark the points on the horizon where the sun rose and set at different times of the year. Such markings served to pinpoint the beginning and end of important periods in agricultural life and permitted the elite priestly class to calculate or predict the coming of important events. From this crude beginning, there could develop a well-organized calendar for determining "holy" or "lucky" days for planting or harvesting crops—a matter of vast importance to people dependent on agriculture for their survival.

Ruins of ancient astronomical formations are known from England, northern France, and other parts of the world. None rivals the Nazca tracings in scale, frequency, or complexity.

For Kosok, the markings in the coastal desert of Peru represented the "largest astronomy book in the world." He was determined to read it.

In the few remaining weeks he had to spend in Peru, Kosok flew over the entire area, obtaining high quality aerial photographs and taking directional readings. He located at least a dozen other "radiating centers." Some of the lines had solstitial direction, as he had expected, but many appeared to have other astronomical significance. Given time, he thought, he could unravel the riddle of the giant Nazca drawings.

Commitments at home called him back to the United States; he would not be able to return to Peru for more than five years. In the meantime, he turned over his information to Dr. Maria Reiche, a Lima-based mathematician-astronomer who had expressed keen interest in his work. Since that time, Dr. Reiche has become a passionate (some say fanatical) advocate of Kosok's original theory.

Dr. Reiche lives, for at least part of the year, in a simple adobe hut at the edge of the desert where she can observe the rising and setting of the sun over the ancient Nazca lines. In this way, she has managed to verify the solstitial nature of the lines plotted by Kosok. In addition, she has found new correlations between the tracings and many other heavenly bodies. Obviously, the enigmatic desert tracings were not built in a random fashion but were designed to align with specific positions of the sun, moon, stars, and planets.

For Maria Reiche, the mysterious Nazca drawings represent an immense desert calendar by which these Indians marked the passing of the years. Like Kosok, she would find special meaning in a passage by the early Spanish chronicler Cieza de León, who wrote: "These Indians watched the heavens and the signs very constantly." Maria Reiche has done the same.

Dr. Kosok remained in frequent contact through the mails, then returned to Peru to resume his field work in 1948. Once again, his time was limited by obligations at home. But until his death in 1959, he continued to collaborate with Dr. Reiche in attempting to organize and interpret the chaotic network of etchings on the surface of Peru's coastal desert. Together, they mapped and computed hundreds of astronomical correlations—and walked hundreds of miles to trace the outline of blurred geometric figures.

It is only the beginning. Still to be explored are hundreds of lines and "roads" that are not related to the solstices and equinoxes. These may have served as sight lines for the rising and setting of the moon, planets, or important stars. Or they may not represent sight lines at all, having served instead to connect related astronomical markings.

And the many lines and figures have not yet been satisfactorily dated. Radiocarbon techniques, so often relied upon by archaeologists to determine the age of prehistoric ruins, cannot be applied to stone. So far, only one radiocarbon date has emerged from the Nazca sites; this date—A.D. 500—was obtained from the remains of a tree stump found at the end of one of the long, narrow lines. There is no way of knowing how long similar etchings had been under construction before this piece of wood was erected as some sort of marker. We know only that the gigantic desert drawings are at least 1,500 years old.

Since the death of Dr. Kosok, Maria Reiche has worked alone. Her devotion to the project is unparalleled, her energy apparently boundless. For nearly thirty years, she has pored over complex aerial photographs, directional readings, and astronomical calculations. Almost singlehandedly, she has fended off highway engineers and land developers who would destroy the ancient desert tracings. On occasion, she has flown strapped to the outside of a low-flying plane in order to take photographs from just the right angle.

And still the mysteries remain. The hundreds of lines which lack astronomical correlations have not been explained. Were these built to represent astronomical configurations not yet considered? Or did they serve as footpaths along which ancient priest-astronomers led religious processions on ceremonial days?

What of the squares, triangles, trapezoids, and rectangles? These immense geometric forms are too precise to result from the accidental crossing of solstitial lines. Could they have served as sacred enclosures in which religious rituals—now lost in time—were performed? The largest geometric figures measure 500 feet wide and more than 1,000 feet long. Hundreds, if not thousands, of worshippers could have gathered within their boundaries. Perhaps they were intended as open-air temples; near some of them have been found large stone heaps—possibly the remains of altars. No one has yet excavated these; perhaps they do, after all, contain human burials.

Most perplexing, however, are the animal shapes and rambling spirals. These, hundreds of feet in diameter, are found closely associated with a wide Nazca line or geometric figures. Most are formed by a single continuous line or narrow path that loops and twists over the desert's surface to depict some animal figure.

Why would hard-working desert farmers go to such lengths to make immense outlines of whales, spiders, flying pelicans, and other creatures? Do the fantastic animal shapes represent prehistoric totemlike symbols intended to honor some favorite animal spirit? Or were they offerings of art never meant to be seen by man—but dedicated instead to the ever watchful Indian gods who looked down upon the earth from their homes in the skies?

And how do the mysterious markings of Nazca relate to similar figures produced by prehistoric peoples of North America? Giant effigies are known here also, from the parched desert near Blythe, California, where crude, childlike sketches of men and horses

sprawl across the landscape. In the Mississippi Valley, huge ser-
pentlike earth mounds were constructed by tribes who occupied
the area in the centuries before Columbus.

Did there occur, at some time in the distant past, contacts between the peoples of North and South America—contacts that permitted the spread of native religious ideas and of techniques used
in building sacred constructions? Or are these scattered effigies
products of independent invention, the result of home-grown
customs whose origins have been lost?

Many of the baffling animal shapes traced across the coastal

Plate 10. Pottery jug from Nazca Valley, dating from A.D. 400–700. Figures
similar to these, found on ancient regional pottery, are duplicated in large
scale across the desert's surface in southern Peru. *(Photo courtesy Organization of American States)*

desert of southern Peru are similar to those found on ancient Nazca pottery unearthed in the immediate vicinity. If the Ica-Nazcas repeated the same designs again and again, in pottery and across the landscape, the forms must have had great significance to them. But what?

The history of the Nazca markings is yet to be fully reconstructed. We are left with too many unanswered—perhaps unsolvable—questions. Perhaps the long lines did indeed serve to determine appropriate dates for planting and harvesting of crops. But the curious spirals and puzzling animal shapes are more difficult to explain.

However energetic future investigations in the Nazca Valley, these desert etchings may remain perplexing.

The Vanished Maya

At the time of the Spanish Conquest, the Incas boasted an elaborate calendar system—one possibly derived from the strange markings so laboriously etched into the desert's surface by early agricultural tribes of the Ica-Nazca Valley.

Long before the rise of Inca civilization in Peru, however, there flourished in the dense jungles of Central America a prehistoric Indian race whose startling achievements in the fields of astronomy and calendrics surpassed those of all other peoples of their time.

These were the classic Mayas, builders of a brilliant and isolated empire that developed and declined centuries before the arrival of the first European in the New World.

Little is known of their origins, even less of their sudden and mysterious disappearance. So far, archaeologists are able to sketch only the broadest outlines of the Mayas' brief but spectacular history.

We know that more than 2,500 years ago scattered bands of Central American Indians began to move into the heart of Guatemala's sweltering rain forest.

It was an inhospitable region. Even today, the landscape is a wild and untamable tangle of towering cedar, mahogany, and palm; needle-spined liana vines wind and loop their way through choking vegetation to impede travel. Venomous snakes, poisonous scorpions, and vampire bats abound. Torrential rains rob the soil of its richness, and drain away so quickly that potable water is always scarce.

In these unlikely surroundings, early Indian settlers built simple thatch-roofed huts. Felling trees with crude stone axes or killing them by girdling their trunks, the earliest human inhabitants cleared enough of the jungle to permit the harvesting of a few meager crops—and supplemented their diet of maize and agave with meat of wild peccary and forest deer. They had no metal tools, no beasts of burden, no wheeled vehicles of any kind. Nor were they destined to acquire such luxuries later.

Nevertheless, their descendants would build, over a span of ten centuries, a remarkable civilization still unparalleled in artistic and intellectual genius.

Guided by demanding gods and powerful central authorities, the Mayas erected massive carved temples, giant causeways, and soaring pyramids to rival those of ancient Egypt. Maya civilization, tended by an elite corps of astronomer-priests, reached full bloom around A.D. 700 and found its greatest expression in spectacular stone monuments that rose like prehistoric skyscrapers above the jungle canopy.

The Mayas were masterful builders who fashioned the most distinguished and innovative architecture in the pre-Columbian New World. Driven by a powerful need to honor their gods and living rulers through ceaseless and insatiable building programs, they labored over hundreds of years to erect and refine their elaborate temples, palaces, and plazas. In their frenzy to build and rebuild, they judged few structures to be complete. Often, they encased old pyramids within newer ones—and did so again and again until the original architecture was hidden inside a maze of multilayered superstructures. As many as twelve times they plastered over the floors of their vast paved courts and open plazas. For the Maya, religion and construction were two sides of the same coin. So long as there were gods to honor, there would be structures to build and rebuild.

The Mayas were also obsessed with time. Through centuries of astronomical observation, they learned to calculate and record the movements of the heavenly bodies and to predict both solar and lunar eclipses. They devised a complex calendrical system by which they measured time with astonishing precision. Although they had no way of expressing decimals or fractions, they kept records so accurate that they could account—at any given moment —for the discrepancy between their year of 365 days and the true solar year of 365.2422 days. Concurrently, they kept track of an elaborate ceremonial calendar that ran only 260 days.

The complexities of timekeeping were known only to the great astronomer-priests; the ordinary Maya farmer or laborer would have had no understanding of the sacred time counts. Yet, for all Mayas, time was of critical importance. They believed that history repeats itself in endlessly recurrent cycles; in order to forecast and prepare for the future, it was necessary to measure the passage of time with absolute accuracy. Each day, each week and month and year, were gods who held the power of life and death over the simplest Maya farmer. The demands of each deity had to be met if the crops were to thrive and the rulers were to enjoy good health and fortune.

And so the Mayas willingly accepted the dictates of their learned ruler-priests. Generation after generation, laborers toiled in the sweltering heat to cut and haul stone for the great temple-pyramids, to stave off the ever encroaching jungle, to plaster and replaster the walls of the secret shrine rooms otherwise visited only by the highest priests.

To honor their multitudinous time gods and to record the reigns of the great astronomer-priests, the Mayas erected thousands of stone stelae, or monuments, inscribed with complex hieroglyphs and sacred dates. The earliest stela so far recovered was carved in

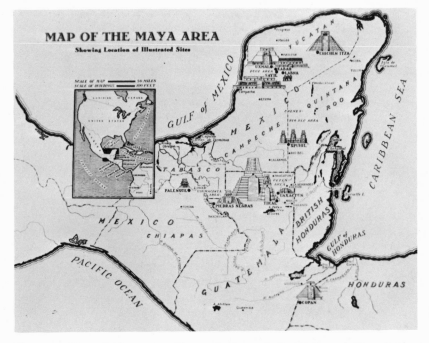

Figure 4. Map of Maya area. *(Courtesy Carnegie Institute and Organization of American States)*

A.D. 279; the most abundant ones date from the seventh through the ninth centuries.

By then, Maya civilization, holding sway in the heart of Central America, was a kaleidoscope of life equaled nowhere else in the New World. There was no dominant capital: Mayadom was a loose federation of scattered city-centers, each with a unique character of its own. Tikal, largest and perhaps the oldest of the ancient Maya cities, was dominated by steep-sided pyramids that faced each other across a broad open plaza. Covering more than 6 square miles, this spectacular prehistoric city must have been a bustling, clamorous urban center where young men vied to train for the priesthood and laborers worked endlessly to expand and refine the ceremonial buildings. In contrast, Copán appears to have been a cultural center; its symmetrical buildings and vast paved ball courts hint at an orderly and serene life style based upon the pursuit of new knowledge and a dutiful interest in the

Plate 11. Ball court at Copán, Honduras, dating from about A.D. 300 *(Photo courtesy Peabody Museum, Harvard University)*

sacred games. Such restraint and tranquility was not reflected at Bonampak, where native artists covered temple walls with brilliant life-sized murals depicting ceremonial festivities and fettered captives.

Whatever their regional differences, the classic Maya cities were bound together by a common dedication to the gods. In every city-center, from the third to the ninth century A.D., the ruler-priests demanded ceaseless construction of sacred temples, palaces, and pyramids—and armies of workers rushed to meet the demand.

And then, for reasons that have eluded archaeologists for more than 200 years, the remarkable Maya Empire collapsed. In the ninth century A.D., all building ceased. No more stelae were erected. The great jungle oases, some still in the course of construction, were deserted. One by one, the cities fell silent. The Mayas suddenly abandoned their sacred temples and pyramids, leaving them to be reclaimed by a wild and relentless jungle.

A few survivors lingered on—at least for a time—about the

deserted plazas, trying in vain to prolong a vanished way of life. Then they too moved on. Year by year the lianas crept closer until the great stone cities, shrouded in vegetation, were lost from sight.

Later, a revived Maya civilization surfaced to the north, in the wilds of the Yucatán peninsula. But this Mexican-influenced variation bore only a little resemblance to the older centers to the south. By the time the first Europeans reached New World shores, the classic Maya Empire, representing the peak of American cultural development, was but a dim memory.

The Spanish, distracted by the thriving cities of Central Mexico and Peru, paid little heed to the ruins of a long-dead empire in the dense rain forests of Middle America. Early American archaeologists were similarly disinterested in the ancient lowland cities. Drawn to the dazzling antiquities of Egypt and Greece that were then being explored, most seemed unaware that remarkable New World ruins awaited their attention.

Among these men was John Lloyd Stephens, a New Jersey attorney, whose hobby and personal passion was archaeology. Stephens had traveled through Greece, Turkey, Arabia, Egypt, and Palestine to explore famous Old World sites. It was not until 1836, when he was thirty-one years old, that he realized he had overlooked a unique prehistoric civilization within his own hemisphere.

Stephens had come across a military report that described strange stone ruins in the wilds of Guatemala. The report was brief and exceedingly dry, offering scant information. But it was sufficient to propel Stephens deep into Central America. He took with him his friend Frederick Catherwood, a skilled draftsman whose precise sketches of prehistoric architecture are admired even today.

As mentioned earlier, the two men plunged into the heart of a country torn by a bloody three-way civil war and narrowly averted disaster when they encountered an aggressive band of drunken soldiers. On muleback, dodging snakes and rival armies, they crossed into northern Honduras to find Copán a majestic ruined city whose monumental buildings and elaborate sculptures exceeded Stephens' wildest expectations.

Quickly they ordered up a labor force and, with machetes, set to work hacking away at the matted vegetation that clung to the ruins—only to be challenged by a native who announced that he was the owner of the land on which the ancient city stood. Startled, Stephens chased the man out of camp.

But the determined little mestizo, Don José María, returned a few days later to insist upon his proprietary rights. Eager to get on with his work, Stephens promptly purchased the entire city—a priceless collection of pre-Columbian art and architecture—for $50.

"There was never any difficulty about price," Stephens wrote later. "I offered that sum, for which Don José María thought me only a fool; if I had offered more, he would probably have considered me something worse."

It took two weeks of grinding work to tear away the jungle's tentacles and reveal the full extent of Stephens' discovery. The artistic wealth of the ancient city was immeasurable. There were palaces, plazas, ball courts, and pyramids; carved jaguar heads and sculptured figures littered the landscape. And there were immense stone stelae, ornately carved and covered with hieroglyphic inscriptions.

Copán was but the beginning. Stephens and Catherwood moved on into Guatemala, Chiapas, and Yucatán, finding along the way numerous other previously unreported Maya sites. By the end of their long and productive trek through the Mesoamerican* wilderness, they had explored forty-four ancient cities. In 1842, Stephens published his *Incidents of Travel in Central America, Chiapas, and Yucatán*. The book, abundantly illustrated with Catherwood's masterful sketches, captured the attention of scholars throughout the world.

Maya civilization, lost for more than a thousand years, had at last been rediscovered. Scattered throughout the lush tropical forests of Central America lay the ruins of a brilliant empire distinguished from all others by its unparalleled achievements in mathematics, astronomy, and architecture—yet based upon a primitive and rudimentary system of agriculture.

The ruined cities abounded in unsolved mysteries, riddles that simultaneously demand and defy explanation. What was the na-

* Mesoamerica is the region extending from north-central North America to Nicaragua.

ture of the people who built these centers of civilization? Why did they choose to settle in this dank and hostile environment?

How did the Mayas, who possessed tools so crude that they might date from the European Stone Age, manage to fashion art objects so sophisticated in design and execution? What spark of native genius ignited the culture that developed the abstract concept of zero while other New World peoples had no counting system at all?

Why did the Mayas abandon their jungle citadels at the peak of their cultural development? Where did they go? Millions of Mayas had lived in these elaborate stone cities. What happened in the ninth century A.D.?

A century of intense investigation has yielded few answers. At a time when Aztec and Inca cities are succumbing to systematic archaeological assault, the Maya cities remain aloof and enigmatic. Although interest in the ancient Maya settlements ran high around the world, few early archaeologists managed to reach the interior cities. Those who succeeded in making the torturous mule-and-machete journey through the rain forests came away dismayed and unsatisfied, their questions unanswered. Even the briefest stay at a ruined Maya city was a nightmare of discomfort and frustration. Most archaeologists slept with guns in their hands, waking periodically to search their blankets for coiled snakes or to listen to the night calls of pumas and jaguars who prowled the darkness nearby. In the rainy season, neither travel nor excavation was possible. In the dry season, a chronic water shortage plagued workers who labored in the steaming heat. To clear tangled vegetation from the crumbling ruins, heavy equipment was needed—but none could be brought in over such rugged terrain.

For some, the privations of research in the jungles of Central America proved too severe. Teobert Maler, a brilliant German scholar who photographed and described dozens of new archaeological discoveries, became convinced that others were profiting from his sacrifices; bitter and disgruntled, he withdrew, refusing to permit the publication of his most recent maps and reports.

In 1863, Spanish scholars at the Royal Academy of History in Madrid stumbled upon a 300-year-old book that would shed some light on the mysteries of the vanished Maya. Entitled *Account of*

Things in Yucatán, the volume had been written in 1566 by Diego
de Landa, the zealous Spanish archbishop who ruled Yucatán
after the Conquest. Historians hold de Landa responsible for the
near-total destruction of Maya literature; it was he who ordered
the sixteenth-century book-burnings in which thousands of original Maya writings—judged by de Landa to be "words of the
devil"—perished. For archaeologists at least, de Landa partially
redeemed himself by leaving behind his own account of life
among the Mayas. His book, describing daily activities in the
postclassic cities of Yucatán, sheds no light on the more ancient
classic centers. But de Landa had included sketches of Maya
hieroglyphs, together with Spanish translations, which made it
possible for experts to decode the inscriptions that adorned the
scattered Maya monuments.

De Landa's book was an important discovery—one that gave
scholars their first colorful insights into the everyday lives of the
mysterious Mayas. From de Landa's account, nineteenth-century
investigators learned that the living sixteenth-century Mayas
looked very much like the sculptured figures found among their
most ancient monuments; that they pierced their ears and noses
and tattooed their bodies; that Maya women painted their faces;
and that crossed eyes were considered by all to be marks of great
beauty and distinction. In fact, Maya mothers were so anxious to
raise cross-eyed children that they fastened small balls of wax to
the forelocks on each child's head, permitting the ball to swing
before the child's eyes. Invariably, both eyes would focus on the
swinging ball; eventually, the child would be cross-eyed.

De Landa also noted that, whereas Maya men were often
promiscuous, their women were expected to remain chaste; it
was a double standard common enough among the invading Europeans and need not have surprised the archbishop. It was the duty
of each Maya woman to produce as many children as possible.
Indeed, if a woman remained barren, she might be divorced by
her husband; on the other hand, if she died in childbirth, she was
honored as a tribal heroine. Aside from her child-rearing duties,
the typical Maya housewife spent her time cooking, cleaning,
weaving, and making pottery. Meanwhile, her husband paid his
"work tax" by laboring in the maize fields or in the cities to build

the great sacred temples and plazas so incessantly demanded by the ruling astronomer-priests. Wealthier men, if we are to believe de Landa, frittered their days away with more pleasant pursuits: playing dice or bean games with their cronies or flirting with other women in the market place.

De Landa, of course, was more a historian than a gossip monger, and he devoted the bulk of his book to the complexities of agriculture, trade, and religion in Maya society. By painting a vivid picture of a people obsessed with time and construction, he revealed for the first time the extent of the Maya genius. In Central America at the time of the Spanish Conquest, there lived a race of people whose vanished ancestors had bequeathed them an extraordinary heritage in mathematics, astronomy, architecture, and engineering.

Now corps of determined scholars swept into the Maya homeland, making repeated attempts to reach, clear, and map the scattered ruins of the great classic cities. They were rewarded with tentative, tantalizing glimpses into the Central American past. Their initial reports hinted at artifacts and structures that—if only they could be recovered—might help unravel the riddle of the classic Maya Empire.

Plate 12. Carved lintel from Piedras Negras. *(Photo courtesy University Museum, Philadelphia, and Organization of American States)*

Plate 13. Uxmal: Temple of the Magician. *(Photo courtesy Barcachano Travel Service and Organization of American States)*

Plate 14. Uxmal: sculptured temple walls. *(Photo courtesy Mexican Government Tourist Department)*

At Tulum, the great walled city that stands on a limestone cliff facing the open sea, investigators found spectacular painted frescoes depicting the various Maya gods; at Piedras Negras, lively life scenes dominate the numerous carved stelae, lintels, and altars. In vivid contrast, Copán was an orderly cultural and intellectual center; here hundreds of stone jaguars guard a complex central acropolis, and more than 2,500 intricately executed hieroglyphs adorn a single massive stairway. Uxmal, considered from the moment of its discovery to be the most beautiful of the Central American cities, boasts the largest of Maya buildings. The House

Plate 15. Mural from Bonampak. The dignitary at top center appears to be giving orders for the ceremonial festivities. *(Photo courtesy United Fruit Company and Organization of American States)*

of the Governor and its related structures, once headquarters for Stephens and Catherwood, cover almost 5 acres of ground.

Bonampak, hidden in a sea of dense jungle, went undiscovered until 1946 and then yielded a wealth of archaeological treasure. Inside its stuccoed buildings, huge polychrome murals serve as a prime source of information about ancient Maya costumes, customs, and life ways. In one building, three rooms of wall paintings show the Mayas in scenes of classic importance: conferring with their priests, conducting raiding parties, taking and passing judgment on enemy captives, offering sacrifices to their gods, and celebrating sacred festivals.

Palenque, discovered in 1832 by a European nobleman who deliberately falsified his sketches to give the impression that this great Maya city had been built by seafaring Romans, was visited again and again by avid explorers. But it was not until 1951 that the city surrendered its most remarkable secret. In that year, a sharp-eyed Mexican archaeologist named Alberto Ruz Lhuillier noticed the faint outlines of a large stone slab set into the floor of

Plate 16. Ruins at Palenque. *(Photo courtesy Mexican Government Tourist Department)*

the pyramid known as the Temple of the Inscriptions. Lhuillier raised the slab, following a narrow stairway downward for more than 60 feet.

There he discovered a magnificent Maya tomb, the first ever to be found within a New World pyramid. At its entrance lay the skeletons of six Maya slaves, apparently sacrifices chosen to accompany their master into the dark afterworld. Over the tomb itself had been placed a massive, elaborately carved stone slab weighing more than 5 tons. And inside lay the bejeweled skeleton of some great but nameless Maya ruler. At his death, he had worn a jade necklace, earrings, and a single large pear-shaped pearl.

Even in 1951, only the simplest equipment and meagerest supplies could be carried in over the rugged jungle terrain to the isolated Maya cities; large-scale archaeological investigations proved impossible. Ruins and artifacts abounded, but the mystery of the sudden ninth-century desertions remained unsolved.

Then, in 1956, archaeologists at the Museum of the University of Pennsylvania joined with the Guatemalan Government to launch the most ambitious archaeological campaign ever attempted in the Americas. Project Tikal—designed to excavate and restore an entire Maya city—was born.

All ancient Maya cities are rampant with unsolved mysteries; Tikal—long abandoned, large and imposing, virtually unlooted—contained more than most. Its excavation was an unprecedented undertaking, one that required building a half dozen new roads and a major airfield, clearing acres of tangled forest, raising more than 1.5 million dollars from public and private sources, and the cooperation, over a fourteen-year-long excavation program, of scientists and governmental officials from two nations.

The project was intended to accomplish far more than the gathering of prehistoric artifacts. Tikal was to provide the raw material for a permanent field laboratory where students and scholars in Mesoamerican archaeology might conduct research and test their hypotheses.

If possible, investigators at Tikal would discover the reason for the city's mysterious ninth-century abandonment—but not at the expense of prehistoric structures that must be preserved in their original condition. To ensure the economic survival of the site

Plate 17. Tikal: partially reconstructed Temple of the Giant Jaguar, which dates from A.D. 700. One of the richest of all Central American tombs was found inside. (*Photo courtesy Organization of American States*)

and field laboratory, it was necessary for workers to restore Tikal with a direct eye to attracting tourists. A modern museum would be established near the site to house the finest artifacts and relics recovered in digging. And the founding of a 222-square-mile national park—the first in Central America—would guarantee the survival of flora and fauna that have flourished here since the peak of Maya civilization, centuries before European discovery of the New World.

In short, Project Tikal was planned to result in the most spectacular tourist exhibit in the world—and, simultaneously, to provide an ongoing center for archaeological research in a meticulously preserved natural environment. It was a tall order: workers would tread a precarious path between systematic excavation, necessary for the acquisition of new knowledge, and aesthetic preservation, mandatory for the growth of tourist traffic.

Because it was the custom of the Mayas to cover older structures with newer ones, archaeologists at other Maya centers had razed many buildings in order to reconstruct their complex histories. At Tikal, only a few buildings—those too badly ravaged by time, weather, and choking vegetation to permit restoration in any case—would be so sacrificed. Carefully planned and laboriously executed lateral tunnels produced an informative cross-section of the city's history. The bulk of the major structures and ceremonial plazas would be consolidated and restored.

Restorations were carried out in exacting detail. Workers at Tikal located and reopened ancient Maya quarries to obtain stone needed for repair or replacement of damaged building façades. They burned limestone for slaking, mixing it with crushed stone —just as the Mayas had done—to produce mortar. Such operations were time-consuming. But they revealed as no theoretical reconstruction could the vast amount of time and energy expended by Tikal's inhabitants as they erected their towering structures of stone.

When primary field excavations ground to a halt in 1966, workers at Tikal had mapped six square miles of the central city. More than 3,000 separate constructions—pyramids, palaces, private residences, temples, shrines, ceremonial platforms, terraces, ball courts, and causeways—were revealed. Some 500 separate excavations had been made, including almost 350 buildings and innumerable human burials, some with rich grave offerings. Hundreds of thousands of archaeological specimens had been uncovered.

Restoration and conservation of the ruins, now under the guidance of the Guatemalan Government, continues to this day. At the University of Pennsylvania, museum researchers anticipate yet another decade of laboratory study, primarily writing and collating field reports. The work at Tikal initiated in 1956 has really just begun.

From the millions of facts collected at Tikal, a rough history has already emerged. Archaeologists tell us that there were people living at Tikal as early as 600 B.C., and perhaps earlier. The city grew and flourished during the classic Maya period—from A.D. 200 to 700—and, toward the end of this period, Tikal's lost inhabitants erected their most remarkable monuments. The Mayas abandoned the city just prior to A.D. 900, at the time when Mayas throughout the empire were deserting other cities of stone.

The intensive, multifaceted investigations at Tikal have produced a myriad of new facts that combine to answer an assortment of old questions, among them the seemingly inexplicable reasons for selecting this remote and inhospitable site for their city.

Why did prehistoric Indians choose to build in this land of torrential rains and prolonged droughts? Apparently, they were attracted to the site by its natural elevation above surrounding swamplands and by the local abundance of high-quality flint, useful in the manufacture of stone tools and implements. They solved the water problem by digging huge reservoirs; the same ones are used today by visitors to Tikal.

Another old mystery centers on the nature of the city itself. Was Tikal, in fact, a city in the true sense of the word? Or did it serve only as an elaborate ceremonial center dedicated to the gods and reserved for an elite corps of priestly attendants? This is a question asked of every sizable Maya site. But at Tikal it has been answered. Excavations revealed an abundance of domestic dwellings. Tikal in its prime housed a wealthy upper class within the city proper; here were located the residences of the priests, princes, artists, musicians, and mathematicians who ranked high in the social hierarchy. Laborers lived in thatch-roofed houses near the outskirts of town, and scattered throughout the nearby jungle were the crude huts of farmers. There can be no doubt that Tikal was a major ceremonial center. But it also housed a heterogeneous population differentiated into classes on the basis of social status and occupation.

Studies at Tikal indicate that the Mayas here maintained extensive trading ties with other classic centers, importing great quantities of obsidian, pyrite, hematite, and jade for making ceremonial objects and jewelry. Sting-ray spines and oyster shells, found in tomb and grave offerings, tell us that Tikal's ancient inhabitants enjoyed sound trading relationships with coastal peoples. And throughout the site comes new evidence of Tikal's close ties with central Mexico, especially with Teotihuacan, that dominant culture center northeast of Mexico City. Not only did the Mayas at Tikal accept pottery styles and trade articles from Mexico, but they evidenced a surprising willingness to commemorate various Mexican gods on their sacred stone monuments. The exact nature of Tikal's ties with Mexico is not yet known. But it is clear that in the fifth century A.D., Tikal's peoples were highly receptive to influences from Teotihuacan.

A few archaeologists have argued that the pyramids of Central America point to prehistoric contacts with Egyptians who somehow crossed the uncharted Atlantic. For prehistorians, it is an unpopular but persistent theory, one traditionally frustrated by the assertion that American pyramids, lacking inner tombs, are only superficially similar to the Egyptian structures. The magnificent royal tomb at Palenque, in the Usumacinta Valley, proved an important first exception; others emerged in the course of excavations at Tikal. Four tombs, dating from the early classic period, were uncovered here. In one, the principal figure is surrounded by carved jade and accompanied by two youths whose sprawling positions indicate that they died in the burial chamber. Below the temple of the Red Stela, workers found a rich burial of an adult male. He, too, is surrounded by elaborate funeral offerings, and nine other individuals—probably sacrificed retainers—accompany him in death. This is not to suggest that such

Egyptian-style entombments prove prehistoric transoceanic contacts. But they do raise some fascinating possibilities.

The greatest puzzle of all remains unsolved. After more than a decade of intensive investigation, archaeologists cannot yet account for the mysterious abandonment of Tikal or of the other classic Maya sites.

There is little evidence to suggest that violent earthquake activity drove the Mayas from cities that had taken hundreds of years to build. The lowlands of Guatemala are located far from the principal earthquake belt, and the destruction of certain Maya structures appears to have resulted not from earthquake or volcanic action but from the corrosive action of time and encroaching vegetation.

Some suggest that the Mayas of the classic period were decimated by yellow fever or malaria. But neither of these diseases is known to have existed in the New World before the time of the Conquest.

It has also been suggested that the depopulation of classic Maya cities came about as a result of soil exhaustion, and it is possible that the Maya system of slash-and-burn agriculture did deplete the soil sufficiently to cause famine in one or more of the classic cities. In others, like Copán, the soil is so fertile and well watered that a mass desertion cannot be explained on the basis of agricultural failure.

Nor is there evidence to suggest that unknown enemy Indians from Mexico or elsewhere vanquished the lowland cities. Limited warfare, consisting primarily of small raiding parties intended to gain slaves or subjects for human sacrifice, was commonly conducted by the classic Mayas. But large-scale warfare is virtually unknown in the Central American lowlands. On the whole, the classic Mayas appear to have been remarkably peaceful. Because they were interdependent among their neighbors for trade, only rarely were their cities protected by defensive walls. The isolation of the great ceremonial centers must have discouraged any would-be attackers.

Perhaps the most plausible theory is one of internal rebellion, and some archaeologists postulate a widespread peasant revolt. In center after center, classic Maya civilization seems to have been the product of an elite class of astronomer-priests with the labor of millions subject to their control. Perhaps the lower classes arose in protest, driving the priests from their sacred temples—then, lacking both leadership and guidance, drifted slowly away from the great stone cities. We can only speculate; no one knows for certain.

It may be that as researchers continue to collate vast masses of information, putting each fragmentary fact in chronological perspective, an answer may emerge; or some extraordinarily fortunate blow of the excavator's pick will unearth a spectacular clue that will serve as a key to unlock the riddle of the vanished Maya.

On the other hand, the past is a jealous mistress. Despite the greatest archaeological assault ever mounted in the Americas, classic Maya civilization is still an enigma.

6

The Caves at Mystery Hill

Mayadom holds a special fascination for archaeologists. Its fabulous ruined cities—jungle-ravaged but intact after more than a thousand years of neglect and isolation—are compelling lures. But Central America has no corner on prehistoric mysteries. Archaeological riddles also abound within the borders of the continental United States.

Etched into the surface of the sun-baked desert near Blythe, California, are dozens of gigantic sand drawings similar to those of southern Peru—and equally mysterious.

At Poverty Point, in northern Louisiana, vast terraces and strange earth hummocks are neatly arranged in concentric circles. No one knows who built them, when, or why.

In the Ohio and Mississippi valleys, giant effigy mounds—some containing tombs—ramble across the landscape to form, in low relief, the outlines of birds, beasts, reptiles, and man. These, too, are the work of a vanished race—one whose prehistoric purposes are lost in the shifting sands of time.

But more mystifying still are the curious man-made caves at Mystery Hill. In the rugged hardwood forest of southeastern New Hampshire lies a jumbled assemblage of megalithic ("great stone") structures. Here, on a wooded hillside, huge granite slabs and capstones—some weighing as much as 75 tons—rest in elaborate disarray to form crude ramps, plazas, subterranean passageways, and cell-like huts. No one knows who pried and levered the heavy granite slabs into place, or why the builders labored to erect this strange stone village. Even the date of construction remains in dispute. After more than thirty years of investigation, archaeologists can agree on but a single point: Mystery Hill may forever defy explanation.

Whoever built this rambling stone complex followed no blueprint and knew or cared little about linear measurements. The mortarless structures mass clumsily and haphazardly together, as if

Plate 18. Mystery Hill: plaza area. *(Photo courtesy Robert E. Stone)*

built by whim. Yet, obviously, most were designed to serve specific purposes, and some were constructed with special care. Numerous rooms have an efficient stone drainage system; one features ingenious stone louvers clearly intended to regulate chimney ventilation.

Dominating the site is a massive granite slab some 10 feet long and 6 feet wide, and weighing nearly 5 tons, which balances atop five crude stone legs. The table is waist-high and ringed by an inch-deep grooved channel with a spoutlike drain-off. Could it have served as an altar for blood sacrifice in some prehistoric rites? No one knows for certain.

Directly behind is located Y Cavern, the largest and most impressive of the structures at Mystery Hill. Roofed with a single granite slab, the three-sectioned chamber contains a fireplace with dampers and smoke hole, a stone bed or altar, and an 8-foot "speaking tube" that leads to the area of the sacrificial table. A man concealed in this granite-lined cubical might whisper into the head-high hollow tube, and his muffled words would swell and echo out beneath the sacrificial stone.

Tour guides refer to the Y Cavern as the "Oracle Chamber," implying some vague link with the Greek oracle at Delphi. Most local residents take exception to such dramatic interpretations of the ruins. They are convinced that the weather-beaten structures at Mystery Hill were built in relatively recent times by an eccentric New Englander named Jonathan Pattee, who lived at the site from 1826 to 1848.

For more than a century, the stone complex was known as Pattee's Caves. Some say that Pattee built the granite huts as an underground railway station for fugitive slaves. Others insist that Pattee was a gun-toting bank robber who scattered his loot throughout the ramshackle structures—or an amiable bootlegger who stashed his moonshine whiskey in the cell-like cubicles.

Actually, Pattee was neither bandit nor moonshiner but a prominent and respected villager who was active in community affairs and once served as town treasurer. Pattee's descendants insist that the curious stone ruins were there when Pattee settled at the site. He used some of the smaller stone huts to store vegetables, and penned his sheep in others.

Plate 19. Mystery Hill: archaeologist Robert E. Stone at sacrificial table.
(Photo courtesy Robert Neikirk)

Plate 20. Mystery Hill: side view of sacrificial table.
(Photo courtesy Robert E. Stone)

Did Jonathan Pattee build these megalithic structures on some eccentric impulse? Or did he simply put them to use—as any practical New Englander would—when he settled on the site? Thanks to William B. Goodwin, we may never know the true extent of Pattee's involvement.

Goodwin, a wealthy insurance executive from Hartford, Connecticut, is both hero and villain in the Mystery Hill story. An energetic but careless amateur archaeologist, he became obsessed with the hillside ruins on this first visit to the site in 1937. Within a few months he had purchased title to the acreage, hired a crew of laborers to clear and restore the stone complex, and set to work formulating his own theory as to the origin of the strange structures.

Goodwin decided that the ruins at Mystery Hill were remains of an Irish monastery built by a band of Culdee monks late in the tenth century A.D. Legend has it that in the year 800, pagan raiders from Scandinavia launched a well-planned series of attacks on the Irish monasteries located along the coasts of the British Isles. The invaders' objective was to seize gold treasures in the custody of the Irish monks. So successful were they that the monks fled to Iceland. When the Vikings followed in hot pursuit, the monks fled again, this time to a land they called Hvitramannaland, far across the western seas.

But where was Hvitramannaland? Goodwin was convinced that at least one band of Culdee monks reached New Hampshire, seeking safety and concealment inland, away from the coastal regions where they would surely face more harassment at the hands of the plundering Norsemen. At the site we know today as Mystery Hill, they came upon an abundant outcropping of fine granite and used this to construct monastic cells. According to Goodwin, the triple-chambered Y Cavern served as the quarters of the Abbot, leader of the transplanted order; other monks occupied the smaller, adjacent cells. From these Spartan quarters, individual monks went forth to convert the Indians of the region. Goodwin located some fifteen additional ruins in New England, all similar in design and architecture to the structures at Mystery Hill; these, he guessed, were outposts used by missionary monks as they battled to bring Christianity to the Indian savages.

In the Norse sagas, Goodwin found reference to the capture, on the American mainland, of Viking explorers by white-robed, white-skinned men who had red beards and spoke Irish. Taking this as corroborating evidence, Goodwin ripped into the site at Mystery Hill, digging furiously for artifacts that would prove the validity of his hypothesis. A crew of local workmen—none trained in the techniques of archaeological excavation—assisted. They uncovered hundreds of artifacts, many dating from the time of the Pattee occupation. But because these failed to prove his theory, Goodwin tossed them away in disgust.

In his frenzy to find evidence of the presence of tenth-century monks, he ignored the most basic of archaeological principles. An archaeological site is a very fragile environment, highly vulnerable to accidental manipulation or destruction. Normally, soil is removed an inch at a time, then screened by hand to catch tiny fragments that might escape the naked eye. Each artifact is photographed, catalogued, and recorded as to its exact location and position before removal. Nothing is discarded.

Goodwin took none of these precautions. Where others might proceed on hands and knees, probing their way into a site with toothbrushes, Goodwin leaped in with pick and shovel. When he found accumulations of silt and air-borne dust—positive evidence that would permit accurate dating of the site in the hands of skilled archaeologists—Goodwin spaded it recklessly away. Anxious to restore the weather-beaten structures to their original condition, he replaced fallen slabs and upended capstones where he thought they might belong.

If scientific evidence for pre-Columbian occupation existed at Mystery Hill, Goodwin destroyed it, not only for himself but also for the generations of scholars who would follow.

Few modern archaeologists accept Goodwin's theory of Mystery Hill as the remains of an ancient Irish monastery. But fewer still are able to offer plausible alternative hypotheses. Most insist that the structures date from colonial times. But what New England farmer would go to such herculean effort to build storage bins for vegetables? And why would he crowd them together in such a haphazard fashion?

In 1955, archaeologists Gary S. Vescelius and Junius Bird directed a six-week archaeological dig, sponsored by the Early Sites Foundation, at Mystery Hill. They found nothing to indicate that the site had been occupied before colonial times. But one bit of evidence did emerge to suggest that Jonathan Pattee could not be responsible for the building of the strange stone huts. Vescelius found a decayed white-pine stump that had grown in soil piled against the wall of one of the cell-like structures, and scientists estimated that the tree had begun to grow from a seedling some-time between 1562 and 1769. Jonathan Pattee was not born until 1796.

If not Pattee, then who—besides the discredited Irish monks—built the curious granite cells at Mystery Hill? Some suggest that American Indians constructed them. But the Indians of the region are not known to have engaged in such laborious stonework anywhere else. Nor is the architecture typical of known American Indians. The Algonquins may have found and used the Mystery Hill structures in historic times, but it seems unlikely that they built them.

Frank Glynn, past President of the Connecticut Archaeological Society, and Frederick Pohl, a well-known Brooklyn scholar and science-fiction writer, have devised a theory centering on a possible Scottish expedition to Nova Scotia in 1398. No evidence survives to connect these visitors with the structures at Mystery Hill. But many historians have argued that Columbus was a relative late-comer to America (certainly the Vikings beat him here) and that early European voyagers may have returned again and again to New World shores without publicizing their travels. Some believe that Celtic peoples from northwestern Europe established a short-lived Iron Age culture in America, near the Atlantic Seaboard, then died at the hands of marauding Indians.

Could fourteenth-century Scots be responsible for the Mystery Hill megaliths? Glynn and Pohl make a convincing case for the presence in that general region of a Scottish expedition led by Henry Sinclair, the Earl of Orkney, in 1398. But did these hypo-thetical visitors settle at Mystery Hill? If so, why would they have fashioned stone structures of this type?

The answer, again, is unknown. There are those who assign a much earlier date to the complex at Mystery Hill. Some investigators see significant similarities between the structures here and prehistoric megaliths found at various Old World sites—particularly those in Portugal and Malta. Crude stone tools, identical to those recovered in European sites dating from 1000 B.C., have been unearthed. And even today, researchers are investigating possible astronomical orientations of Mystery Hill's "winter solstice monolith." When viewed from the sacrificial table at the very center of the site, this massive upright stone appears to be in alignment with the setting of the sun at the time of the winter solstice—that is, on December 21, the first day of winter. Should results of the investigation be positive, researchers hope to link the structures at Mystery Hill with those at England's famous astronomically oriented ruins at Stonehenge. These investigators theorize the existence of a mysterious group of Stone Age builders—members of the people that raised the gigantic megaliths at Stonehenge, who crossed the Atlantic to duplicate their feat at Mystery Hill.

How could prehistoric men cross so large an ocean? No one can say—but a number of workers at Mystery Hill have searched tirelessly for evidence that the ruins date from the Stone Age.

In May of 1969, members of the New England Antiquities Research Association gathered to dig for charcoal samples suitable for dating by the carbon-14 method. They opened a trench in an undisturbed area, digging to an average depth of 2 feet, or 3 to 8 inches above bedrock. There they unearthed a broken pick, a hammer stone, and a crude stone scraper. Also retrieved from this level was a small sample of charcoal, which was immediately submitted for radiocarbon age determination.

The age of the charcoal fragment, according to technical directors at Geochron Laboratories in Cambridge, Massachusetts, was 2,995 years, plus or minus 180 years as a margin of error. For the first time, workers at Mystery Hill had evidence of occupation dating nearly 3,000 years into the past. If the date proves accurate, Mystery Hill represents the oldest man-made construction in North America.

There has been no rush of archaeologists to support the astonishing antiquity now assigned to the structures at Mystery Hill. But a few noted scholars have lent cautious support. Cyrus Gordon, Professor of Mediterranean Studies at Brandeis University, thinks it possible that, about 1500 B.C., the men of the people who built Stonehenge reached the New World to construct the cell-like structures and erect the grooved table at Mystery Hill.

Members of the New England Antiquities Research Association, led by President Robert E. Stone, look forward to additional

Plate 21. Mystery Hill: archaeologist Robert E. Stone stands at entrance to Tomb of Lost Souls. *(Photo courtesy Western Electric Company)*

research and excavation at Mystery Hill. Disappointed by the negative reactions voiced by more traditional archaeologists to news of the 1969 carbon-14 date, they hope to uncover new evidence of antiquity at the site—supporting evidence that will prove beyond a doubt the validity of the age they claim for the ruined structures at Mystery Hill. They are aware that many of the world's greatest archaeological discoveries have been made by amateurs, and they remain undeterred by the scoffings of professional doubters. Their efforts to unravel the riddle of Mystery Hill, coupled with their strict adherence to sound archaeological principles and their willingness to consult professional archaeologists, have won them grudging admiration from their staunchest opponents. And more than one skilled archaeologist has bolted the opposition camp to join their ranks.

The site may yet yield significant evidence. Chances are equally good that it will not. The damage done by Goodwin's reckless plundering is irreparable; workers can only hope to find the ground undisturbed by Goodwin and his zealous crew.

No matter how old the megaliths, they still must have been known to colonial inhabitants of New Hampshire. Yet there is no mention of them in colonial records; and no local legends, passed from generation to generation, survive to shed light on their origins.

For those who have studied the megaliths, Mystery Hill guards not one secret but two: Who built the cell-like huts? And why do colonial records omit all mention of them?

At Salem, Massachusetts, scene of the seventeenth-century witch hangings, shame prevented the villagers from mentioning the witch trials for many decades afterward. Public records and colonial documents were carefully edited to minimize the terror of the witch craze; modern historians note glaring omissions from the historical records.

Could the stone structures on Mystery Hill have served as a site for occult practices in colonial times? They might have provided an appropriate setting for rites practiced by underground survivors of the Salem witch cult. If so, is it not likely that frightened townspeople would omit all mention of the ruins in public documents?

We can only speculate. The origins and nature of the stone buildings at Mystery Hill have been swallowed up in the passing of time. Barring spectacular new evidence—an archaeological miracle—they may never be revealed.

7

Intruders Before Columbus

William B. Goodwin was neither the first nor the last to suggest that peoples from the Old World reached American shores in prehistoric times. But few have been so imaginative or so energetic as Thor Heyerdahl in their pursuit of proof.

While other, more traditional scholars were content to argue the likelihood of prehistoric transoceanic voyages, Heyerdahl sought to prove it possible that ancient Egyptians conquered the high seas as early as 3000 B.C., landing in the Americas thousands of years before Columbus—and in time to have had a hand in shaping the development of the higher civilizations of Central and South America.

Heyerdahl is no stranger to the sea. In 1947, he sailed from South America to Polynesia aboard the *Kon-Tiki,* a copy of an Inca balsa-log raft, in order to show that pre-Columbian Peruvians could have contributed to Polynesian culture.

Later, he became intrigued with similarities between the ancient cultures of Egypt and America. Like the Egyptians, the Indians of pre-Columbian Central and South America built reed boats, pyramids, and gigantic stone statues. Similarly, both worshiped the sun, married brother to sister in royal families, practiced hieroglyphic writing, and mummified their dead.

Was this a coincidence? Or was it imitation made possible by prehistoric transoceanic contacts? Heyerdahl resolved to find out if the voyage, at least, were possible.

On May 25, 1969, in a 50-foot vessel which duplicated the structure of a papyrus-reed craft depicted in Egyptian tomb reliefs, Heyerdahl staged his departure from the same coastal waters of Morocco that launched Columbus. He took with him six human companions, a monkey, and a duck—and restricted food supplies to those available to hypothetical ancient mariners. By riding trade winds and equatorial currents across the Atlantic to a safe landing on the Yucatán peninsula, they hoped to demonstrate with irrefutable logic that prehistoric peoples had the means to traverse a mighty ocean.

For fifty-six days, Heyerdahl's craft, *Ra I,* rode the waves like a "giant paper swan." Then the curved stern began to sag, and the ship listed to starboard. The crew sacrificed their only life raft, cutting it up and fastening it to the stern for buoyancy. Encircling sharks made additional repairs impossible. On July 12, Heyerdahl and his water-soaked crew reluctantly abandoned ship. They had come 2,700 miles on an epic journey—but fell 600 miles short of their goal.

Undaunted, Heyerdahl traced the failure of the *Ra I* to a basic error in construction. Buduma tribesmen from Lake Chad, commissioned to build the craft, had noted in Egyptian frescoes a rope running from the top of the stern to the deck of papyrus-reed boats; judging the line to be purely decorative, they omitted it when building *Ra I.* Heyerdahl's crew found that the rope would have helped to hold the craft together, just as a bowstring arches and stabilizes a wooden bow. Heyerdahl laid plans immediately for the construction of *Ra II.*

On May 17, 1970, Heyerdahl and a seven-man crew set off in a second attempt to cross the Atlantic. *Ra II,* about 9 feet shorter than its predecessor, featured the previously missing rope. And on July 12—exactly a year from the date *Ra I* was abandoned—this second craft carried Heyerdahl triumphantly into Bridgetown harbor in the Barbados. He had proved that this unlikely vessel—a copy of those used thousands of years ago by the Egyptians—was capable of crossing the Atlantic.

Putting out to sea in a paper boat represents no more than a practical—if venturesome—attempt to solve one of the most intriguing of archaeological riddles: What happened in the Americas before the arrival of Columbus? No one has yet satisfactorily explained the rise of such remarkable New World empires as those of the Aztecs, Toltecs, Mayas, and Incas, where peoples of amazing sophistication developed highly organized communities characterized by achievements often duplicating—and at times surpassing—those on the other side of the Atlantic. Nor have scientists been able to prove or discard the cryptic hints of pre-Columbian contacts between the Old and the New worlds.

At the very heart of the question lies the mystery of how man's creative nature works. We know that the earliest Old World civilizations—the growth centers of ancient Egypt, India, China, and the Near East—were variously interrelated, the development of each one stimulated by extensive cross-fertilization of ideas and innovations borrowed from the others. Scientists have long assumed that human contacts and cultural trading are requisite to the development of higher systems of civilization.

Is it possible that the peoples of Central and South America, living in absolute isolation from the cradles of Old World civilization, developed their incredible empires in isolation? Or must they have been shaped and stimulated by influences carried to them by other peoples who reached New World shores?

Any ocean poses an awesome barrier to the spread of human populations and ideas, and anthropologists have traditionally rejected the notion that prehistoric peoples possessed the means necessary for crossing an unmapped sea. The isolationists argue (and very adequately) that there is no good reason why the peoples of Central and South America, having once unlocked the secret of agriculture, could not have produced their cultural marvels unaided. Man is a creative animal, one prone to invention in response to his needs. What he invents in one hemisphere, he can invent independently in the other, given the same set of needs and circumstances.

And yet certain elements in the higher American civilizations are strangely reminiscent of Old World cultures, among them the very features that so intrigue Heyerdahl: sun-worship cults, hieroglyphic writing, skilled techniques of human mummification, advanced medical procedures, and pyramids that rival those of ancient Egypt at the peak of her splendor.

And these are but a few of the duplications that excite the imaginations of those who would illuminate America's lost centuries. However improbable the ability of prehistoric peoples to navigate the oceans, there is a lot of coincidence to explain away on the basis of independent invention—and there is an enticing abundance of clues to a mystery that may never be solved.

For those who reject the theory of pre-Columbian oceanic voyages, as well as for those who support it, there is little doubt that the initial gateway to the Americas was approached not in ships but on foot. But did other migrations take place between the time of the arrival of the first nomadic Asian immigrants and the coming of the sixteenth-century Spanish?

Archaeological sites seldom escape the notice of cranks, and the higher American cultures make prime targets. Hundreds of fanciful theories have been advanced to explain the rise of the extraordinary civilizations of Central America and Peru over the four hundred years since their discovery. A few of the earliest investigators—if we may call them that—were sufficiently overwhelmed by the region's cultural achievements to suggest that the cradle of life lay not in the Old World but in the New World. But there never existed in the Western Hemisphere any animal form from which man could have evolved. No fossil remains of anthropoid apes—or of ancient species of man—have ever been unearthed.

What of prehistoric land connections? Certainly the Americas were connected, at some point distant in time, to another of the great land masses; science is gradually proving it so. But any direct land links disappeared long before man diverged from his ancestral primate stock.

It is often suggested, even today, that ancestors of the Mesoamerican natives arrived here on rafts from Polynesia or Micronesia, and an increasing number of anthropologists seem willing to discuss the feasibility of Pacific contacts in pre-Columbian times. The Pacific Islands, however, were uninhabited at the time of the earliest Mesoamerican settlements; hence the Pacific Islanders fail to qualify as an ancestral group.

First the Spanish came and theorized—and then the missionaries and archaeologists. Finally, laymen began to prowl the "lost" cities of Central and South America, formulating their own theories. In 1882, Ignatius Donnelly, a Philadelphian attorney, published a book entitled *Atlantis, the Antediluvian World,* in which he claimed that the Mayas, Aztecs, and other New World Indians were derived from colonies sent out from that wonderful but mythical sunken continent. The book, largely occult and filled with errors, remains in print today. Strangely, the Atlantis theory is one of the most pervasive. There is no evidence to support it; geologists maintain that no continent existed in the Atlantic—at least in the last 60 million years—that might have been the legendary doomed Atlantis.

Taking a page from Donnelly's book and reversing it in 1932, James Churchward pinpointed man's creation in the Pacific Ocean, on the mysterious island kingdom of Mu. From secret, sacred tablets he claimed alternately to have uncovered in Tibet or India, Churchward tells of a vast lost continent of 64 million inhabitants—people who colonized the world, beginning with Mesoamerica. Mu, according to Churchward, vanished more than 12,000 years ago in a vortex of fire and water. The story of Mu makes a spellbinding tale. Unfortunately, it contains not a single fact.

For most archaeologists, the same limitation applies to the various theories that attempt to link the peoples of Central and South America with the Hittites, the Etruscans, the ten lost tribes of Israel, and the lost fleet of Alexander the Great. More persistent is the notion, promulgated by such men as Eliott Smith and W. J. Perry, that large populations were transported to the New World from Egypt in prehistoric times. Smith's theories derive from the oft-cited finding of gold in Mesoamerica. According to Smith, gold is invariably symbolic of the sun, the primary ob-

Plate 22. Gold pectoral plate from Tiahuanaco, Bolivia. Objects of gold, like this one, found in New World sites convinced early investigators that Egyptians reached the Americas centuries before Columbus. *(Photo courtesy Dumbarton Oaks, Washington [the Robert Woods Bliss Collection])*

ject of worship not only for the Egyptians but for many American Indians as well; wherever gold is found, the Egyptians could not be far behind. Most modern investigators agree that wholesale migrations of peoples across the seas into pre-Columbian Mesoamerica could not have occurred. The suggestion that such early seafarers could successfully carry huge populations and requisite food supplies over uncharted oceans is almost unthinkable.

But what of occasional Old World contacts—the accidental windswept crossing on troubled seas, the one-in-a-million lucky landing by explorers bent on a far-ranging quest for gold or slaves or virgin land? New World attainments in mathematics, engineering, and astronomy are so sophisticated that they must have taken many centuries to reach—unless, of course, some unknown intruders visited American shores at the dawn of New World development. And if strangers from distant lands did reach the Americas in ships—not in wholesale lots but in sporadic odd boatloads—we would expect to find, superimposed upon the uniquely American civilizations, spotty but obvious traces of Old World contacts.

And this is precisely what we do find. In Mexico, Cortes and his men met Indians who wore helmets—curved, crested ones identical in shape to those favored by the Greeks in the time of Alexander. Coincidence? Echoes of that lost fleet? Or did helmeted men deliberately cross the ocean to land on the coast of Mexico centuries before Columbus?

In Guatemala and Yucatán, where Indian high priests poised at the edges of their sacred wells to practice rites of human sacrifice, early Spanish conquistadors witnessed baptisms, confessions, and penances—an eerie combination of Christian and native ritual. Had some Old World Christian passed here before them?

At Cholula, in Mexico, stand the remains of great pyramids strikingly similar to those of ancient Babylonia. Mesoamerican pyramids resemble only superficially those of ancient Egypt. In detail they more closely approximate the structure of Mesopotamian ziggurats. Both are truncated, forming the base for an upper temple; both feature steep outside staircases that rise to the very top. The Tower of Babel was a ziggurat; so is the pyramid at Cholula.

The Mesoamerican pyramids triggered the concept of prehistoric connections between Egypt and the New World. They also provided one of the classic arguments used in opposition to that concept, for the pyramids of the New World are hardly analogous to those of Egypt. Not only do these differ in structure, but the pyramids of the Nile Valley were constructed as tombs, whereas those of Mexico and Guatemala were erected as bases for temples and were not used as depositories for sepulchers. The latter argument collapsed in 1949 with the discovery of a tomb in the Temple of the Inscriptions at Palenque, in the classic Maya region. It was here that Alberto Ruz Lhuillier located an underground funeral chamber, hidden deep within a maze of structural detours and false passages—much as in the tombs of Egypt—designed to frustrate intruders. The inner chamber obviously was meant to house the bodily remains of a high priest or chieftain, for the crypt offerings include the finest jade, pearl, and gold. Moreover, the crumbling skeleton itself is heavily adorned, with rings, bracelets, and a beaded breastplate. Over his face, in the Phoenician fashion, lay a mask of jade, fragmented and arranged in a moasic pattern. Near the skeleton, archaeologists recovered a small jade idol, apparently intended to represent Kinich Ahau, the Mayan sun god. Strangely, the figure carved in jade depicts not the clean-shaven, Mongoloid features one would expect of a Mayan idol but those of a bearded face—one with a convex nose more familiar in the Old World than in the New World.

The sarcophagus itself is monolithic and huge; more than a few man-hours were spent laboring over the task of hewing out the rounded head and flared base. Both are strongly reminiscent of Phoenician sarcophagi that were modeled, in turn, after Egyptian mummy cases. The damp stone coffin rests in its inner chamber as if guarded in the Egyptian fashion, for in the outer chamber rest the remains of six individuals. Apparently, these were servants sacrificed so that they might accompany their master on his journey to the other world—a practice most common, again, in Egypt. Is this another string of coincidences?

If so, they are found in the company of even more bizarre phenomena. For the bearded god found in the crypt at Palenque recurs throughout Mesoamerica. Aztec legends tell of a white, bearded god who brought the gift of knowledge and then departed, promising that his brethren would return one day. This great white god is Quetzalcoatl; his likeness and that of his alternate form, the feathered serpent, recur widely throughout Central America.

Legend is exceedingly difficult to trace. As I have mentioned, the Mayan books that might have distinguished fact from fiction were destroyed shortly after the Spanish Conquest. Did Quetzalcoatl once live in mortal form? This much is certain: his home and capital, the ancient Toltec city of Tula, exists. As for the recurring fair and bearded representations, they appear at numerous sites, always with features that bear little resemblance to the Mongoloid face we would expect to find.

We might of course discount the nose and suggest that the un-

known bearded god was Mongoloid after all. In ancient Egypt
pharaohs unable to raise luxuriant beards often resorted to artificial ones; perhaps rulers in Mesoamerica succumbed to the same
vanity. But we are left with the question of origin: Who is the
bearded figure who inspired such repetitious sculptures?

To complicate matters, the fair, bearded god is not the only
alien face with which archaeologists must contend. For there appears also in Mesoamerica a face strongly Negroid in character—
at a time in a land where the presence of African peoples cannot
be explained. At numerous sites in Mexico, archaeologists have
excavated dozens of colossal heads carved from single blocks of
stone. Most are at least 6 feet tall, are more than 18 feet in cir-
cumference, and weigh more than ten tons; several specimens
loom even larger. The unbroken blocks of stone from which they
were carved were somehow transported—by natives who lacked
both wheels and domesticated animals—from quarries up to 10
miles distant. The faces on these immense stone heads seem inescapably Negroid.

Racial features even in the living are often deceptive. Can we
be certain that the carved heads are intended to depict the presence of Negroid peoples? The answer, of course, is that we cannot.
But at Monte Alban, in Oaxaca, were uncovered great rock carvings, on blocks used in building construction, that feature dancers
with markedly flat noses, thick lips, and round faces. These are
hardly representations of the Indians who carved them—if the
sculptors were indeed Indian. Together with the carved dancers
appears, once more, the nameless bearded god whose dominant
convex nose seems so curious in Indian America.

If no black men lived in the New World before the coming of
Columbus, how can archaeologists account for these figures? Western scientists and historians have long argued that no African
peoples possessed, during that distant era, the means to make a
journey to the New World. A few have theorized a storm-driven
African craft landing accidentally on the coast of Mesoamerica.
Others think it possible that the slave-trading Carthaginians, returning from raids along the African coast, were driven west by
storms to land in the New World with their slave cargo. Does the
bearded apparition so often associated with the Negroid carvings

Plate 23. San Lorenzo site, Veracruz, Mexico:
colossal head in course of excavation.
(Photo courtesy Robert Squier)

Plate 24. Santiago,
Veracruz, Mexico:
colossal head on
display.
   *(Photo courtesy
Robert Squier)*

represent some luckless sea captain gone astray with his human cargo?

An increasing number of historians, following a trail pioneered by energetic black scholars, find it unnecessary to postulate such theories. Legrand H. Clegg II, historian for the African-American Historical Association, summarizes a position that is rapidly gaining advocates:

> A reservoir of evidence has come to our attention regarding the apparent existence of black peoples in the Americas during the ancient (*circa* 3,000 B.C.—?) and medieval (*circa* 500–1500 A.D.) periods. Remote Indian and African legends; ancient and medieval skeletal remains and sculptural discoveries in the Americas; black American colonies sighted by sixteenth-century European navigators as well as the personal testimony of Columbus, Balboa, and other early European explorers have caused more than one anthropologist to conclude with Carlos C. Marquez that "long ago the youthful America was also a Negro continent."
>
> Whence came these curious blacks? Hasty conclusions cannot be drawn. Yet we know that from the cultural morning of inner Africa until the twilight of the Moorish regime, the Mother Continent produced civilizations of advanced maritime achievement. Of major note were the ancient kingdoms of Egypt, Nubia, Ethiopia, and perhaps the Nok culture of Nigeria—all extending over a period from *circa* 3,100 B.C. to 500 A.D.; as well as the medieval nations of Mali, Songhay, and the Moorish "empire."
>
> Some scientists have further theorized that the black Sabaeans of southern Arabia, the Dravidians of India, as well as the early Melanesians may have scoured the seas and reached the New World in ancient times. A number also insist that black Australoids pioneered the trek over the Bering Strait and into the New World. Finally, a few historians have held that the seafaring Phoenicians and their Carthaginian offspring (both of whom may have reached the New World) were of black extraction.
>
> Although most of the foregoing theories remain essentially in the fetal stages, we are prepared to say that, according to strong circumstantial evidence, West African navigators from Mali and Songhay and Blackamoors from Spain or North Africa almost certainly crossed the Atlantic and reached the Americas during the Middle Ages. J. A. Rogers even suggests that Columbus may have learned of the New World from these black explorers.

Despite the inevitable sifting, interpreting, and classifying which must transpire before we, as Pan-African historians, dare additional hypotheses, we are currently agreed upon one central point: that black people *from somewhere* were apparently present in the New World from the pre-Classic epoch until the onslaught of European explorers.*

Not long ago, Clegg's statement on the possible presence of Africans in the pre-Columbian New World would have been met by the academic community with hoots, glares, and scorn. Even today, a number of scholars refuse to accept the notion of *any* alien influences in prehistoric America.

But we can no longer dismiss evidence that Africans may have sailed to the New World before Columbus. New knowledge of the navigational capabilities of prehistoric Africans may turn the tide of popular opinion, with Clegg and his colleagues finding ardent new support. In the meantime, the curious colossal heads and dancing figures from Mexico cannot be ignored.

For Professor Cyrus H. Gordon, the evidence points toward pre-Columbian visitors from the Mediterranean. Reassessing a palm-sized, inscribed stone tablet found eighty-five years ago in a Tennessee burial mound, Gordon argues that Jews fleeing the Romans in the Middle East may have discovered America at least a thousand years before Columbus. The Bat Creek Stone appears to be inscribed in the style of Canaan, the Israeli promised land located somewhere between the Jordan River and the Mediterranean. According to Gordon, circumstances of discovery rule out the possibility of forgery or fraud. Still, Gordon has found little support for his claims among archaeologists. Even newspapers— notably the *Jewish Observer* and the *Middle East Review*—ridicule his suggestion that the inscribed stone tablet was of Palestinian origin.

But who can say for certain? Opponents of the various transoceanic-contact theories argue that had there been Old World settlers in the Americas before Columbus, archaeologists by now would have unearthed their skeletal remains. Yet all ancient human skeletons recovered in the New World have been judged

* Personal communication.

racially homogeneous; that is, all seem to represent the type we know as American Indian.

Only a tiny fraction of living populations, however, die or are buried under conditions favorable for future discovery. And the range of human variation is so great that scientists are hard pressed to define racial characteristics in the living; racial identification on the basis of skeletal remains alone is especially difficult. Objective anthropologists insist that we cannot be sure that no Old World skeletons have been found in the Americas.

The ambiguity of the skeletal remains severely limits their value in solving the mystery of possible intruders before Columbus. But paintings, sculptures, and pottery representations that depict the human face and form are available for study. On the basis of terra-cotta pottery recovered in Central and South America, Alexander von Wuthenau, lecturer at the University of the Americas in Mexico City, argues that not one but several Old World races were represented in the pre-Columbian New World. Von Wuthenau has collected from museums and archaeological sites a dazzling array of facial types drawn from ancient Indian pottery. Some, including a recently discovered Mixtec head, appear unmistakably Negroid; others look Semitic. The almond-eyed Olmec figurines seem inescapably Asiatic. Other figures—especially those from Nayarit, on Mexico's Pacific Coast—look remarkably like modern-day Chinese.

What Indian artists are responsible for this gallery of international faces? And who served as artists' models?

There remain to be explained an endless inventory of cultural "coincidences," for Mesoamerica abounds with objects that cannot be accounted for. Archaeologists puzzle over a recurring lotus motif, widely encountered in both India and Central America. They ponder the unexpected appearance of bark-beaters, which were used in making bark cloth at the time of the Conquest; similar bark-beaters are found in the Pacific, where they are made of wood, and in Asia, where they are made of stone and wood. The Stone of Tizoc, found among the remains of Aztec culture, is remarkably similar to objects found in Macedonia and Babylon. Spindle whorls unearthed in Palestine and Egypt can scarcely be distinguished—even by experts—from those found in Mexico and

Peru. Peruvian looms, both of the horizontal and the vertical types, duplicate those of Egyptian origin from 1900 B.C.—down to the identical number and arrangement of working parts.

And the New World also presents features that echo the works of Southeast Asian cultures. The Chac-Mool, a famous reclining god common in later pre-Conquest times in Toltec and Maya sites, appears widely in Indian and Southeast Asia from early Buddhist eras. Ear spools from Cuicuilco, Mexico, and copper bells from Chichén Itzá, Yucatán, are identical to objects common in excavation sites in Southeast Asia. Most startling of all is the discovery, in Cambodia, of Angkor Wat, the fabulous lost temple that is the most Maya-like of all Old World constructions. It is simple enough to dismiss a handful of copper bells; there are, after all, only so many ways to construct a bell. But it is more difficult to dismiss duplication of architecture throughout an entire city. For those seeking to link transoceanic cultures, the city seems compelling proof of cultural connections and seems a persuasive argument for pre-Columbian contacts.

Such inventories soon become overpowering and dull. Duplicated objects lose their excitement when included in an endless cataloguing of cultural traits. However, duplications in craft techniques provoke sustained fascination.

And we do find such duplications. Not only were the various techniques of metallurgy—plating, welding, smelting, soldering, forging in copper, gold, silver, platinum, and lead—known in the New World many hundreds of years before Columbus (and thus far without evidence of a long history of experimentation such as is found in the Old World), but also archaeologists encounter that intricate procedure of casting known as *cire perdue*, or "lost wax." In this method, the maker first models in clay, then wax. Over the whole he applies more clay, leaving at the base an opening through which the melted wax may flow when the object is heated. Into the same opening the craftsman then pours molten gold, or some other precious metal, to replace the lost wax. When the metal is set, the outer casing is broken away to reveal a perfectly modeled, single-piece product. The earliest peoples to cast metals in this fashion were the Toltecs, the Incas, and the Phoenicians.

In Peru, methods of water conduction—irrigation and terracing—were identical with those used in the agricultural regions of Mesopotamia and Egypt. Peruvian quarrying and construction techniques duplicate almost exactly ancient Egyptian procedures.

Numerous traits in pre-Incan Peru—mostly inscriptions and characters found in pottery, sculpture, and metalwork—seem to have Oriental overtones. A few investigators have professed to link dozens of words in Peruvian dialects with the languages of China and Japan. But the similarities seem superficial and far-fetched to those who oppose the theory of pre-Columbian contacts.

Much more suggestive of early contact is the incised pottery from Valdivia, Ecuador, found by Clifford Evans and Betty Meggers of the Smithsonian Institution and by the Ecuadorian Emilio Estrada. The pottery, dating from about 3200 B.C., is amazingly similar to pottery made during the same time period in Japan.

Might favorable winds and ocean currents have carried the occupants of a Japanese fishing boat to the coast of Ecuador in pre-Columbian times? Perhaps. Still, no concrete evidence yet exists to suggest that there occurred any long or continuous contacts between the Old and New Worlds in prehistoric times. And most archaeologists agree that there is no single period in American archaeology when massive cultural influences, carried by sizable migrations, reached New World shores.

How much "coincidence" is needed to constitute proof of alien intruders in the Americas before Columbus? How many "duplications" are sufficient to dismiss the probability of parallel cultural evolution?

For most experts, much more comprehensive evidence is required than has been uncovered so far. Subjective comparisons of individual cultural elements easily yield apparent duplications. Too often similarity, like beauty, is in the eye of the beholder.

The fact is that advocates of the various transoceanic-contact theories have failed to construct a unified coherent body of evidence in support of their contentions. They are unified only in their common insistence that outside influences played a crucial role in the development of the great New World civilizations. They cannot agree as to the nature or specific origins of those influences. Some look to Egypt as the "mother culture" from which the higher New World empires sprang. Some trace the many cultural parallels between Southeast Asia and Central America. Others argue for the prehistoric presence of Africans—or Mediterraneans or Orientals—in the New World. And still others cling to the unlikely theory that a potpourri of intruders reached pre-Columbian America, making the prehistoric New World a veritable melting pot of races. As a result, the diffusionists leave themselves vulnerable to challenge from those who continue to view the native American cultures as autonomous ones.

Too often advocates of the diffusionist position have been rightfully judged guilty of haphazard research or slipshod scholarship. Many of them, dazzled by apparently significant cultural duplications, have failed to inquire into the meaning of "similar" traits in their separate contexts—and as a consequence have watched their "evidence" come tumbling down about their ears. Peru's red-haired mummies, cited as proof of prehistoric contacts between Egypt and Peru, furnish upon closer investigation no evidence at all. First, the procedures of mummification in Egypt differed markedly from those in Peru. Second, the red hair is not a genetic heritage but a chemical reaction to the burial environment.

Other investigators blithely ignore the significance of time. Heyerdahl's Atlantic crossing was indeed a spectacular feat. But this swashbuckling Norwegian adventurer-archaeologist failed to consider the most basic question relevant to his hypothesis: If ancient Egyptians carried a sun-worshiping culture across the Atlantic in 3000 B.C., why is it that elements of sun worship do not appear in the American archaeological record until 1,500 years later?

Even today, the greatest obstacle to acceptance of the theory of prehistoric transoceanic contact remains the improbability that any Old World group possessed the means or the motivation to undertake such a perilous voyage. An ocean, after all, poses an awesome barrier to human travel. It seems superfluous to point out that the crossing of *Ra II*, dramatic as it was, proved only that an experienced captain and a knowledgeable crew could sail a reed vessel across the Atlantic in modern times. It did not prove that a similar vessel might have managed the risky trip in 3000 B.C. Nor does it support in any manner the contention that ancient Egyptian sailors did indeed make the journey.

There are additional obstacles. On the whole, lists of presumed cultural duplications make flimsy evidence for prehistoric contacts. Any competent archaeologist can present a good case against circumstantial evidence. Who can judge the prehistoric significance of similar lotus motifs or wooden ear spools? Must they constitute evidence for human contacts—or is it just as likely that they provide examples of parallel evolution or mere coincidence?

Nor does the bulk of these apparent duplications strengthen the case for prehistoric contacts. For, if we were to count up all the known Old World–New World duplications, we would net an impressive array of them, but we would also have to contend with some awkward omissions.

One of the major arguments against the possibility of transoceanic contact revolves about the noticeable *absence* of certain important Old World culture traits in the New World. Whenever peoples meet, they exchange ideas and inventions. Had Old World groups invaded the New World in ancient times, we would expect to find evidence of a sharing of their most important inventions. Yet there seems to have been no knowledge in early America of the true wheel. The only wheels so far discovered have been those found on small objects believed to be children's toys. If Old World aliens did indeed reach the New World, why did they fail to introduce so obvious and important an invention for use in agriculture and architecture?

Diffusionists answer that there was an abundance of cheap human labor in the New World—and no need for the wheel. This seems a weak and unconvincing argument.

And they offer no explantion at all for other striking omissions, including certain important Old World food plants, knowledge of iron, and use of the true architectural arch. It is very strange indeed that hypothetical aliens would fail to introduce into America such critical culture elements.

And so we continue a controversy that has raged for nearly 300 years. It seems impossible to build a strong case for prehistoric transoceanic voyages. And yet there are those recurring and inexplicable echoes of other civilizations thriving oceans distant.

There are no easy answers. Most experts are cautious. Because the evidence for Old World aliens is circumstantial and unsatisfactory, they look for more concrete proof. One approach centers about the compilation of mutually exclusive lists of cultivated plants indigenous to the Old and New worlds. Early travelers would have carried with them food supplies, the seeds of which would have bridged the botanical gap between the continents. So far, most of the botanical evidence is inconclusive. But this potentially critical evidence needs to be re-examined with modern techniques and without bias.

The Bering Strait theory remains secure. There can be no doubt that it was by this route that the earliest Americans entered the New World. Their descendants peopled North America, then drifted southward to settle in Central and South America.

Here, perhaps, they were joined by strangers from across the seas—not by the lost tribes of Israel or the mythical inhabitants of Mu, but by yet unnamed men who came in ships. There were no wholesale crossings, no boatloads of people who arrived to import their Old World cultures. But there may indeed have occurred occasional contacts, be it by design or by accident.

Traditional archaeological resistance to this notion is crumbling. And this is the significant point, far more so than the presence of individual artifacts or the absence of specific culture elements. Pitfalls still abound in segregating the proved from the probable in American archaeology. But archaeologists who a decade ago would have dismissed the notion of early transoceanic contacts accept the hypothesis today as debatable fact. They stress the need for flexibility of acadamic positions to permit the modification of views as new evidence accumulates.

We now wait for that accident of preservation, that whimsical turn of fate that guides a spade to the proper site at the proper time to reveal the undeniable footprints of vanished aliens—if such intruders did walk here in ancient and forgotten times.

Epilogue

The past, it is said, is more difficult to predict than the future. The fragmentary evidence for man's cultural prehistory is hidden in the earth, often in remote, unlikely regions where only the most dedicated archaeologists—or the most intrepid amateurs—venture to search for knowledge of past human life.

Clues to the course of human development are meager. Only a fraction of man's material culture survives the ravages of time, climate, burial, and encroaching vegetation. A still smaller fraction is found and recovered, and even less can be fitted with accuracy into the puzzle that is human prehistory.

Despite the limitations imposed by the eccentricities of accidental preservation and discovery, archaeologists have succeeded in weaving for us a rich tapestry of past human achievement. Mysteries remain, to be sure, and only a few of them have been discussed in this book.

It is remarkable that scientists have reconstructed as much of the past as they have. To piece together the facts of prehistory is a laborious task. Archaeologists in the field work under conditions few day laborers would tolerate. In isolation, with pick and shovel or with toothbrush and trowel, they toil in the dim hope of grubbing up some fragmentary prize, which may or may not provide a clue to man's life in ancient times. For there are no guarantees in archaeology.

Why dig? Why—when the earth shudders with the problems of the present—do men and women pursue the past with such fervor?

The answer that leaps most quickly to mind has to do with curiosity. We are beasts born hungry for knowledge, especially as it concerns ourselves and our origins.

But there are also practical reasons for resurrecting the past. If we are to understand our present nature, we must know the nature of our ancestors. If we are to know where we are going, we must first learn where we have been. Whenever and wherever we live, we are part of a great ongoing process, which triggered and now sustains the biological and cultural evolution of man and his animal relatives.

Two worlds collided when the first conquistadors invaded the American mainland. What implications can we draw from that disastrous encounter?

The Maya world collapsed five centuries before Columbus, for reasons archaeologists have yet to reconstruct. But, if the cause was overpopulation, or soil exhaustion, or revolution, there are lessons to be learned here, too.

And in archaeology, just as in the modern space program, there are often spin-off benefits to be gained. When Thor Heyerdahl and his crew crossed the Atlantic in their papyrus-reed craft, they spotted new, previously undetected signs of oceanic pollution—and sounded an alarm heard around the world.

Who can estimate the benefits to mankind to be derived from a better understanding of human behavior and of the origins and development of cultures and civilizations? The prehistoric New World presents us with a vast natural laboratory. It is here that we might best explore the significance of varying rates of cultural evolution.

What factors trigger and sustain the process of cultural evolution? How is it that one or two human groups may develop rich and progressive civilizations over a span of a few hundred years while neighboring groups barely manage to sustain themselves with a crude and limited culture?

Must we explain the rise of the great American civilizations by hypothesizing a transplantation of Old World ideas, social forms, and inventions? Or did the impetus come through some chance invention indigenous to the Americas?

What factors set the stage for the development of great civilizations? Have these to do with diet, or natural resources, or climate? Or does the chance development of a particular social organization or ideology predispose a given people to greatness?

If we can discover why some peoples advanced beyond others in the ancient Americas, we might apply this knowledge to the betterment of life among the people of modern emerging nations.

If we can isolate the seeds of greatness in pre-Columbian Mesoamerica, we might be better qualified to shape modern priorities. What factors, for example, were the significant ones in the classic Maya culture—the use of complex social institutions in governing large populations, or the more esoteric achievements in art, architecture, and astronomy? If we had answers, might we not be in a better position to examine our own culture and to encourage and support the development of culture elements that could lend stability to our own society?

If we can reconstruct the history of the early New World, might we not be able to understand more about the rise of the state in other parts of the world—and at other times?

Even in our rushed and frenzied world, it is unthinkable for us to fail to pause occasionally for a look backward. In the artifacts so laboriously collected in archaeological excavations, there are to be seen intimations of the thoughts, hopes, and strivings of our vanished predecessors. Theirs is a shadowy world, but one that casts a glow of human achievement.

For those who track that compelling light, today's mysteries are tomorrow's revelations.

For Further Reading

Chapter 1. THE EARLIEST AMERICANS

BURLAND, COTTIE. *The People of the Ancient Americas.* London and New York: Paul Hamlyn, 1970.

HOLE, FRANK, and ROBERT F. HEIZER. *An Introduction to Prehistoric Archeology,* 2d ed. New York: Holt, Rinehart and Winston, 1969.

JENNINGS, JESSE D., and EDWARD NORBECK (eds.). *Prehistoric Man in the New World.* Chicago: University of Chicago Press, 1964.

SPENCER, ROBERT F., *et al. The Native Americans.* New York: Harper & Row, 1965.

Chapter 2. MACHU PICCHU: LOST CITY
IN THE CLOUDS

BENNETT, WENDELL C., and JUNIUS B. BIRD. *Andean Culture History,* 2d ed. New York: Natural History Press, 1960.

BINGHAM, HIRAM. *Lost City of the Incas.* New York: Atheneum, 1963.

DE LA VEGA, GARCILASO (ed. by Alain Gheerbrant). *The Incas.* New York: Avon Books, 1961.

Chapter 3. THE RIDDLE OF THE TREPANNED SKULLS

BROTHWELL, D., and A. T. SANDISON. *Diseases in Antiquity: A Survey of the Diseases, Injuries, and Surgery of Early Populations.* Springfield, Ill.: Charles C Thomas, 1963.

JANSSENS, PAUL A. *Palaeopathology: Diseases and Injuries of Prehistoric Man.* London: John Baker, 1970.

WELLS, CALVIN. *Bones, Bodies, and Disease.* New York: Praeger Publishers, 1964.

Chapter 4. THE MYSTERIOUS NAZCA MARKINGS

DEUEL, LEO. *Flights into Yesterday.* New York: St. Martin's Press, 1969.

KOSOK, PAUL. *Life, Land, and Water in Ancient Peru.* Brooklyn, N.Y.: Long Island University Press, 1965.

Chapter 5. THE VANISHED MAYA

COE, MICHAEL D. *Mexico.* New York: Praeger Publishers, 1962.

COE, WILLIAM R. *Tikal: A Handbook of the Ancient Maya Ruins.* Philadelphia: The University Museum, University of Pennsylvania, 1967.

COTTRELL, LEONARD. *The Horizon Book of Lost Worlds.* New York: Dell Publishing Co., 1964.

MORLEY, SYLVANUS GRISWOLD. *The Ancient Maya,* 3d ed. Stanford, Calif.: Stanford University Press, 1956.

Chapter 6. THE CAVES AT MYSTERY HILL

POHL, FREDERICK J. *The Lost Discovery.* New York: W. W. Norton and Company, 1952.

ROBBINS, ROLAND W. *Hidden America.* New York: Doubleday & Company, 1959.

SLOANE, HOWARD N., and RUSSELL H. GURNEE. *Visiting American Caves.* New York: Crown Publishing Company, 1966.

TAFT, LEWIS A. *Profile of Old New England.* New York: Dodd, Mead & Company, 1965.

Chapter 7. INTRUDERS BEFORE COLUMBUS

HONORÉ, PIERRE. *In Quest of the White God.* London: Hutchinson & Co., Ltd., 1963.

IRWIN, CONSTANCE. *Fair Gods and Stone Faces.* New York: St. Martin's Press, 1963.

VON WUTHENAU, ALEXANDER. *The Art of Terra-cotta Pottery in Pre-Columbian Central and South America.* New York: Crown Publishing Company, 1969.

WAUCHOPE, ROBERT. *Lost Tribes and Sunken Continents.* Chicago: University of Chicago Press, 1962.

Index

DATE DUE

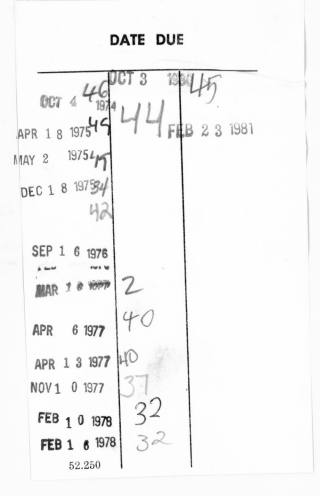

OCT 3 1980 45

OCT 4 46 1974

OCT 4 46 1974 44

APR 1 8 1975 45 44 FEB 2 3 1981

MAY 2 1975 45

DEC 1 8 1975 34

42

SEP 1 6 1976

MAR 1 6 1977 2

APR 6 1977 40

APR 1 3 1977 40

NOV 1 0 1977 37

FEB 1 0 1978 32

FEB 1 6 1978 32

52.250